THE SUGAR JAR

YASMINE CHEYENNE

HarperOne
An Imprint of HarperCollins*Publishers*

THE
SUGAR
JAR

*Create Boundaries, Embrace Self-Healing,
and Enjoy the Sweet Things in Life*

HarperCollins books may be purchased for educational, business, or sales promotional use. For information, please email the Special Markets Department at SPsales@harpercollins.com.

FIRST EDITION

DESIGNED BY BONNI LEON-BERMAN
ILLUSTRATIONS BY MELARIE ODELUSI

Library of Congress Cataloging-in-Publication Data has been applied for.

ISBN 978-0-06-316236-5

10 9 8 7 6 5 4 3 2 1

To my Gma, thank you for supporting
my wildest dreams without hesitation.
I miss you always.

To Mari and Yara, always feel free to be you.
I love you always.

CONTENTS

AUTHOR'S NOTE

Anytime you commit to starting something new, there's bound to be a variation of changes, lessons, gifts, and maybe even some growth discomfort. I wrote this book to offer you many invitations to explore yourself and your healing journey in ways that you may not have considered before. Through my own stories, and the stories of others, I hope this book reminds you that we're not as alone in our experiences as we think we are. With that in mind, I encourage you to affirm to yourself, in this moment, that you are willing to take this opportunity to approach this new journey with ease, grace, kindness, but also with intention. I also encourage you to take action in this book by underlining what stands out, highlighting what you want to revisit, dog-earing the pages that you want to readily find, "Post-it noting" any words you found powerful and instrumental to your growth in places where you can see it every day when you start your day, and any other ways that will help you begin to integrate this work into your life. Carry this book with you. Use it whenever you need to. I'm so proud of the work you're about to do and all that you've already done to get here. Let's do this!

So much love,
Yasmine

THE SUGAR JAR

PREFACE

I grew up being rocked to sleep by the lullaby of the Brooklyn-Queens Expressway. Cars drove by all day and all night and trucks would hit large bumps in the road, sounding like a huge collision. This all happened right outside my window in Fort Greene, and I was so used to it that when I left New York, I couldn't sleep for a while because of how quiet it was. Sirens and the general noise of Brooklyn streets were a comfort for me. It's such a metaphor for life because the noise, if it's all you're used to, becomes home and the quiet can feel otherworldly and take time to adjust to.

I knew early on that I wanted to create a life for myself that looked very different from what was around me. I was born with the feeling of wanting to create a life that felt as good as it looked. But I also struggled with finding people whom I could relate to growing up. It felt like there were people who were successful because they were really smart or people who were successful because they were really beautiful, and although life is much more complex than those two categories, as a child I bought into the belief that I needed to be a genius or a model to have a good life. This belief stayed with me and because I didn't believe I fell into either category, I worried my dream of a fulfilling life wouldn't come true. Even though I knew I was smart, I didn't carry that knowing with me as if it was a part of me, and isn't that the case sometimes in life? Where we know something to be true about ourselves, but because we don't fully believe it or acknowledge it, we might find it tough to hold on to as a strength we actually possess. One thing I was able to hold on to was that I loved to write and I knew that I wanted to help people, so I committed myself to finding ways I could do that.

A year after graduating from high school, I joined the military to change my environment, but also because at the time I thought it was the only way I could get an education while also having a job. While in the Air Force, I went through training to become a victim advocate for my base and spent two years supporting people who'd been victims of a crime. I helped them navigate through everything from sexual assault to child abuse and domestic violence. Although my job was to primarily help them fill out paperwork in the beginning, I never did just that because I knew they needed more. I felt like there should be resources not only for financial support but assistance to ensure they had access to mental health services as well.

I set out to re-create the way victim advocacy was done on my base and in such a bureaucratic system like the military, I began to connect people to resources throughout the country that helped them gain access to what they each individually needed. I recognized that when people had access and support, anything was possible. I learned that with community I didn't have to have all the answers, I just had to be able to connect people to what they needed. I realized that being able to listen to their stories, no matter how tough their experiences were, provided ease and support to them and I knew it was something I wanted to continue to do. The seed to help others heal was planted in me from that moment. But even then I knew that I would need to start my own healing journey as well.

I began to imagine what life would feel like if I didn't *have* to do anything I didn't want to do. I explored how my life would be impacted if I was able to *choose* what I *Most of us don't know* what our healing journey will change in our lives when we get started. We just hope that the change that occurs creates more ease and peace than we had when we began. said yes or no to. I invited myself to consider what my relationships would feel like if I wasn't doing what I thought I *should* be doing and instead chose only what felt right to me. This honestly felt impossible at the time. Not only did I not know a single person who was living this way, I fully bought into the mind-set that attempting to live for me was incredibly selfish. *What about everyone else and who would be there for them?* I'd always think to myself. But I began to question the idea of that "selfishness" because I knew that the way I was currently serving others wasn't working, so how could I serve myself? What would this look like? I didn't know at the time, but I began and continued the journey of finding out how it would feel for me.

Most of us don't know what our healing journey will change in our lives when we get started. We just hope that the change that occurs creates more ease and peace than we had when we began. We commit to our healing to make room for who we want to be. And to make room for our joy, we're usually invited to clear some stuff out. For me, those first few years of my journey included some tough conversations, big adjustments, and major overhauls. But it also helped me to gain clarity on who I was, stand firmly in what I wanted, and move forward with my intention to teach and support others on their healing journeys.

After going through many immersive trainings as well as a coaching program, I began developing my own way of teaching self-healing. My intention is to empower people to learn how to come back to themselves and remember the power we have to choose what we want while communicating what we need. The lessons shared in this book changed my life, but they've also helped me to teach so many people how to shift their own lives. And even now, when I decide to bravely choose myself, I lean back on these very tools to remind me why it's important to commit to me. I hope this book will be carried with you, highlighted, dog-eared, and tabbed with a fierce knowing that you can start from wherever you are as many times as you need to.

The changes are possible no matter where you're from or where you are in your life right now. The tiny steps you're taking matter.

The big steps you're taking matter. And even though you might be committing to this journey without a bit of certainty, as I know I did, ask yourself: What would it feel like to take a chance on giving myself what I say I want? What would it feel like to not settle in any way? What would my life be like if from this moment on, I chose me in each moment and every way that I could?

INTRODUCTION

I sat at my living room table wondering why I was feeling so overwhelmed with my life, saying to myself, "I've been teaching boundaries for so long. *Why am I* still so overwhelmed?" As I sat there stewing in my to-do lists, my commitments, and my unanswered text messages, I immediately began to think to myself, *Okay, Yasmine, slow down. Let's ground. What do you feel like you need in this moment?* I decided to begin recording a voice memo, which is one of my favorite ways of journaling because there's so much power in speaking how you feel out loud, especially when there's no one on the receiving end to listen. As I spoke, I shared that I felt like sugar that was recklessly taken out of a jar and spilled all over the place. I could sense the parts of me that were spilled, that I'd never be able to find or reclaim. It was interesting because, even though I knew my sugar was in a jar that was supposed to keep my energy safe and the jar served as a boundary to my energy, I also knew that despite these boundaries people still had access to my sugar anyway. As I thought about all of the directions I felt I was being pulled in, I could clearly see that the sugar was in cracks and crevices on the countertop, stuck in the ridges around the jar, and I could also see that the reason people were able to keep coming into my kitchen and accessing my jar was because I was allowing them to by not having a lid on it. My sugar jar was completely open and available for whoever wanted access to me. Even though I told myself that I didn't want to keep overcommitting and people-pleasing, I kept saying yes without truly checking in with whether I had enough sugar to give. I realized that boundaries should go way beyond just my safety and protecting the interactions I had with others and that I needed to reframe the way I set boundaries around my time, my energy, my money, and all the other areas of my life. After having the visual of the sugar jar, I could easily see where all of "me" was going.

I was shocked. "I'm literally all over the place. I need to call my power back to me," I said to myself while frantically looking for a pen and paper to begin to jot this down:

- Say no

- Use your voice

- Give to yourself, too

- Always check within

- Resist the urge to over-give

I stared at the page and said out loud to myself: "I thought I dealt with this. I thought this part of my healing journey was done."

Although I felt overwhelmed by realizing that I was about to revisit an area of healing that I thought I was finished with (and honestly thinking I was "done" should've been the sign to me that I wasn't), I also felt empowered. As a healer, I recognized that if this was coming up again, then I was ready for another iteration of learning. I saw that my sugar jar was damn near empty. And not only that, but there was also a mess on my countertop around the sugar jar, on the floor, and in my whole kitchen. So I got to work, revamping my energetic kitchen and letting in some more light. Cleaning the floor and letting go of the fact that there would be granules of sugar (my energy) I'd probably never be able to reach in certain cracks or crevices. I wiped down the counter, cleaned off the jar, and looked around.

"I need to change the locks or something because not everyone needs access to this kitchen," I again shared out loud to myself. I began writing a list of whom I'd always allow to have access and another list where I'd need to remove access and instead require permission each time. Then I closed my jar and created a plan to refill it at least halfway to begin. I doubled down on scheduling all the things that I knew would rejuvenate me and thus my jar. I also had to cancel and say no to things that I knew would drain all the work I'd just put in. And then I began the over-five-year journey of learning about my sugar, my jar, and my kitchen. What filled me up? What drained me? What experiences in my life caused leaks or cracks? What commitments were using more sugar than I realized? What boundaries did I need to set? Did I even like the color of these kitchen walls? How could I ensure that my jar was the size I needed to feel grounded, safe, and supported? How could I ensure that the atmosphere around my jar, which was my lovely kitchen, would be a place where I always felt safe? When I didn't feel safe, what did I need to learn to be able to speak up or act on my own behalf?

This moment completely impacted me and shifted my life, and after sharing it with others, I realized it was helping them, too. *The Sugar Jar* shows you another way to begin to look at how your energy is being used by yourself and others. Sugar can be used with intention to make many wonderful things or it can be accessed without care and become very messy and hard to manage. The sugar jar journey starts on the inside and eventually impacts all the ways we show up outside ourselves because everything that we need to care for ourselves internally and externally also impacts our jar.

In this book, I talk about tapping into our awareness, saying no to performing, boundaries, parenting, healing as a Black person, and so much more. For each topic, I share insights as to how your sugar jar is being impacted based on the decisions you make and how you can shift your choices to create a life that isn't overwhelming and instead feels like a warm inviting kitchen, with a full sugar jar that is ready to commit and give to everything that *actually* matters to you.

So with that I invite you to ask yourself this question: How's my sugar jar?

1

THE SUGAR JAR

I remember feeling like I couldn't add one more thing to my to-do list. I'd just had a baby, and after my maternity leave ended, I felt like I was immediately thrust from the cocoon that I had created for myself to heal and adjust to my new world of two kids into the real, full-blown calendar-event heavy-hustle-filled world again. I was building my business as a self-healing teacher and writer, and to my surprise it was growing faster than I'd expected. I was excited for the growth but also feeling the weight of everything that needed to be done in every area of my life. I was getting invites for parties, trips, and dinners from every direction. At the time, I felt like "I *should* see this as a good thing, I *should* be enjoying this," which kept me from accessing how I was really feeling in that moment. Even though I was healthy, my baby was healthy, my oldest daughter was thriving, my business was growing, and people wanted to hire me, I was absolutely over-whelmed. I always thought that this kind of busyness and success was when I would feel "full," but instead I was feeling depleted. I didn't understand this at all. I kept asking myself, *Why was this too much? What's wrong with me?* I honestly thought that this was the lifestyle I wanted.

When I had that big moment of actualization in my kitchen about my sugar jar, and I realized that not only was it empty, but it was empty because of my choices, I was at a loss for words. My energy, money, time, resources, space, and ideas, all the parts of me, were being used at the max because I was saying yes to all of it. There was rarely anything left for me. And when there was some of my energy left for me, I was often the one ready to give it away. In retrospect, I realized that having sugar in my jar felt uncomfortable, because having an empty jar was my normal. I was unconsciously always willing to give it away.

This was in complete contrast to the story I was telling myself. My story was that the people who were coming in and out of my kitchen were doing so without my permission and that they were *taking* from me. The truth was that yes, people were coming in and going out of my kitchen, but it was because I left the door open and the lid off my jar. I was allowing them to take, and I was showing up to give when I wanted to say no.

When I discovered my sugar jar, I was in awe of how it helped me to see, understand, and adjust what was working for me and what wasn't. When I think about the things that weren't working for me before that moment, it was often the everyday invites, adulting, and tasks that I'd feel nervous about saying no to because of the potential backlash. Instead of saying no or adjusting my yes based on what I needed, I'd resentfully go along with the plan, thinking that it was the easier option, telling myself the story that it was the person who invited me or presented the ask who was inconsiderate of my time or energy when actually it was my responsibility to be clear with myself on what I needed and then make decisions based on my needs.

For example, let's say I was invited to a friend's party that started at 8:00 p.m. and ended at midnight. Let's also add that the friend shared with me that they were so excited that I was coming and that "their birthday wouldn't be the same" without me there. Before the Sugar Jar, I would've:

- Been excited to be invited but nervous about the time I'd be getting home based on my schedule.

- Worried about how I'd be able to get everything done before I left for the party.

- Probably felt some resentment about how late the party was starting and how I had to be there to not let my friend down.

I would have focused on all the external things taking place rather than looking at what I needed and what I could control within myself. I wouldn't have realized the power I had to put parameters in place that would allow me to care for myself and my family before I went, or that I could decide that I wouldn't be able to make it. I wouldn't have realized how many options I had, and I would've felt trapped by feeling I needed to be what I believed my friend desired me to be for them. Someone else's decision to have a party at whatever time they choose is not a personal attack on our time, but so many of us feel that way when we don't think we have control over our time and energy.

Let's use this same party-invitation scenario after I discovered my sugar jar and began to understand how I could advocate for my needs on a deeper level. Before I even accepted the invitation to the party, I'd stop to assess whether I could easefully attend by asking myself a few questions:

- Is going to this party going to be possible while managing what I've already committed to?

- Is there any way that I can ask for support with anything I've already committed to so that I can go?

- Am I already overcommitted and do I need to decline the invite?

Sometimes we think that because we're going to a party or a dinner or a place where we'll enjoy ourselves, that it's worth it to just go and think about the to-do list later, especially if we're already stressed and overcommitted. And there are so many times when this is true, and it's worth it to just do the fun thing. But then there are many times where we're overcommitted, overwhelmed, and stressed because we always just say yes. And it can be a lesson for us to learn to say no if we really don't have the time or the energy.

After asking myself these initial questions and before I accepted the invite, I would then assess my jar:

- How much sugar do I have?

- Will saying yes fill me or deplete me?

- Do I want to say yes to this?

If the answer is no, then I decline the invitation and perhaps offer another way that I can spend time with them. I'm allowed to feel disappointed that I'm unable to attend. They're allowed to feel how they feel as well about my no. But ultimately, I'm honoring where I'm at, and this is an important part of taking care of ourselves.

If the answer is yes, that I do want to attend, then I look at how I can put boundaries in place with myself so that I can enjoy the party while also managing my jar, aka my needs, with care. It would look like:

- I'm excited to go to this party, but I'm going to let the host know that I'll be leaving by 10:30 p.m. That way I can get home early enough to still get some rest and meet my schedule the next day.

- I'll let myself off the hook with some tasks that I might not be able to complete before I go and find easeful ways to complete them over the next few days. I'll make sure that the things I must do for the next day are done so I'm not overwhelmed.

• I'll remind myself that it's my choice to attend and that I'll need
  to honor my boundaries and leave on time.

Instead of looking at everything from the perspective of "I have
no control," checking my jar reminds me of where I do have control and I can then make decisions from that place. My decision
is what works for me right then and it could change in the future
depending on what's going on in my life. I'm allowing myself the
flexibility to adjust whenever I need to without being a burden
on others or feeling like it's my responsibility to carry others'
emotions about my choices.

You might be thinking, "Who cares, it's just a party!" But
whether it's an invite to a party, a request to take on more work
when you're already overwhelmed, a phone call where you're being
emotionally dumped on, or a request for money that you don't want
to give, we're all asked to do things that upon that immediate ask,
we're unsure if we feel comfortable saying yes. Taking a moment to
figure out how you feel about the ask, and how you feel in general,
can help you be clear about what works for you and what doesn't.
Those "little" requests from the people in our lives add up. One
tablespoon of sugar here and one cup of sugar there—it all adds up.

In the scenario shared above, we covered setting external and
personal boundaries, understanding our emotions, calling our
power back, assessing our time/energy levels, and easeful communication in our relationships. The Sugar Jar became the perfect way
for me to be able to bind all these modalities into one teaching tool.

Sometimes self-healing can feel unattainable because we're wondering, "How am I going to remember all of these tools and know how/when it's appropriate to use them?" But with the Sugar Jar we're able to easefully see our goals, our emotions, where our time is being spent, how our energy is doing, where our finances are going, and how much sugar we have left for ourselves.

The Sugar Jar allows us to easily discern what we need, what we don't, and how we can move forward.

INTENTIONS > PLANS

When I ask, "What's your intention?" I'm interested in your purpose behind why you're doing or committing to what you've chosen. But a lot of times, intention is posed as "What's your plan?" and that usually ignites a very different part of us. Intention connects us to our feelings and sometimes our feelings are different from our plans and goals, which can sometimes cause us to create a life that isn't aligned with what we <u>really</u> want. We sign up to do what doesn't feel great hoping it will eventually lead us to nirvana.

This kind of thinking can also box you into a perspective that once you decide on something, you're stuck with that decision. Even if you're suffering, even if it hurts, even if you know differently now, stick. to. the. plan. no. matter. what. This is where we can be the ones limiting our own freedom of choice, freedom to change our minds, and freedom to grow and evolve.

It's common to get lost in our intentions, plans, and goals because we believe we're doing what we *should* be doing. We don't always feel we have the option to do the things *we want* to be doing. And when it starts to become clear that the "should" we committed to isn't aligned, it can be hard to reckon with the reality that we chose "wrong."

You might feel like you're failing and that might lead to you being hard on yourself. But in reality, you didn't have the awareness about what you wanted before you said yes, or before you loaned the money, or before you went on the date, or before, or before, or before. Wouldn't it be helpful to be able to check in with yourself and ask: "Why am I doing this?" "Why does this feel uncomfortable?" "What was I hoping to gain versus what have I learned is the reality of doing this?" "How can I shift this so that I feel better?"

Well, to help you better understand what you say yes to, whom you say yes to, why you feel drained in certain relationships, and to become more familiar with how much your exchanges with the people, places, and things in your life impact you in different ways, I am going to introduce you to *your* sugar jar.

Your sugar jar will help you figure out why you feel so exhausted even though you felt you were "doing the right thing" for a friend. It helps you learn more about why you always say yes and feel guilty when you say no. It helps you lean into your intuition and figure out why who you've been taught to be may not fully align with who you actually are. Yes, that may feel like a lot, but the truth is that so many of us have been programmed to function in a society that wants more and more of us, without concern for our well-being, which means that we've got to be our own advocates. We've got to be the one to say, "okay, this is enough for now, no more."

Getting to know your sugar jar can also help you understand why you may be feeling depleted, resentful, exhausted, lonely, drained, taken advantage of, or overwhelmed in your relationships. Through understanding our sugar jar, we can see where we put our energy, what we rank as important, what we choose in our lives, and why. Why is this important? Well, because your sugar jar is you—a visualization of your life and all the people, experiences, and attachments you have to every single thing that takes up space in your life. I know, let me explain.

I'd like you to imagine a kitchen that you can see clearly in your mind. It may be somewhere you've gone before, it may be your dream kitchen, or it may be where you grew up. Allow it to be a place that you enjoy visiting and want to visit often. Envision this kitchen with all its utensils, windows, smells, colors, and shapes. You may even have a kitchen that comes into your mind that you've never seen before—this is okay, too. Imagine the countertops in your kitchen, get to know the lighting, the seating, the entryway, and the way the entire space flows. Now I'd like you to imagine a jar of sugar, aka your sugar jar, on one of those countertops. See it in your mind and make sure you've got a good image of it.

Before we go any further, let me explain how your sugar jar works.

YOUR JAR

The jar represents you, meaning your actual body, soul, mind, and the vessel containing all your energy. The jar has the responsibility of holding all of you together, and even though it's strong, it's also fragile. Your jar should be clear glass so that you can easily see from the outside in what's needed.

Although we hold many titles and roles in our lives, we have only one jar because there is only one of us. The jar represents all your titles, whether you're a parent, partner, sibling, coworker, or friend—you still have only one jar. Everyone has a different-size jar, and the size of the jar represents your capacity to give and to receive with all the people and things you're in a partnership or relationship with. Your jar size can be large to hold many friendships, businesses, commitments, and experiences. Your jar could also be smaller and have space for only your closest friends, your career/business, and your partner, and not a lot of space or energy for anything else.

The size of your jar is determined by you, and you can always decide to have a larger or smaller jar as you see fit, perhaps changing your jar size based on where you currently are in your life. When determining the size of your jar, remember that you will have to keep it filled with sugar (we'll talk about sugar in a minute) for all the commitments and people in your life as well as for yourself, so pick a size that feels right to you or keep the size you currently have and as we go through this journey together, you can determine if you'd like a different size.

I also want to remind you again that you get to decide on the size of your jar, and the significant thing I'd like you to become aware of as you decide on your jar size is: Why do I feel excited, nervous, scared, shame, weird, or [insert here] about my jar size? Begin by asking yourself this and building awareness about what comes up for you as you inspect and learn more about your jar size, aka your capacity to hold all the things you have in your life.

For example, do you feel particularly proud to hear that your jar size is large? Why do you think you feel pride about that? Do you feel proud that you have a smaller jar? Why does your jar feel right to you? Do you feel shame about your jar size? Or are you feeling overwhelmed by confirming that your jar has been tough to keep up with? Are you limiting your growth by not realizing your capacity and thus playing it small? Take note of what comes up around the size of your jar, knowing that you don't have to make any decisions or changes right now, just be aware of how it feels and what you feel and why or where you feel this emotion is coming from.

Before we move on to exploring your sugar, I'd like you to imagine again the size of your jar on the countertop in your kitchen. Does anything else in your kitchen stand out? Try to get that picture of your kitchen and the jar as clear as you can in your mind so that every time we go back to it, it easily appears to you.

YOUR SUGAR

Your sugar represents all the sweet parts of you—your time, your energy, your attention, your money, your expertise/education, and every single part of you that can be given or exchanged. Ask yourself: Do I usually offer my sugar, aka my time, attention, money, or support, because I genuinely want to and have enough sugar to give? Or am I offering my sugar because I've been taught that this is what I do to be loved, accepted, seen, cared for, and held? Sugar sweetens so many things, but when it is mismanaged, it can become messy, spilling into crevices that are hard to clean. Have you ever spilled sugar before? It's one of those things that can feel impossible to clean up, and when it comes to your energy being disbursed, that can also feel true.

In addition, when your sugar is being given to too many different people and commitments, perhaps because you don't have a lid on your jar (aka boundaries), people are able to come into your kitchen and grab a teaspoon of sugar here, a cup of sugar there, and as we already talked about it, it gets messy, right? When managed with care, you can ensure you have enough sugar to give to yourself, while also sharing it with everything and everyone that matters most to you.

FULLNESS OF YOUR JAR

When your sugar jar is between three-quarters of the way full and completely full, you're often able to handle life with more ease.

The attributes of a life with a jar filled this way may include:

- Having healthier boundaries.

- Having healthier relationships.

- Giving yourself regular self-care.

- Struggling with guilt after setting boundaries, but able to be there for yourself compassionately afterward.

- Having "free time."

- Feeling like your life reflects your desires.

- Not allowing busyness to keep you from joy.

When your sugar jar is half to three-quarters of the way full, you might still feel like you're able to handle life easefully most of the time, but you may also often feel strained.

The attributes of a life with a jar filled this way may include:

- Making time for self-care after realizing that the stress is piling up.

- Perhaps choosing avoidance over setting boundaries with people out of fear of hurting them and dealing with the potential emotional repercussions.

- Often feeling on the verge of burnout.

- Often feeling like you don't have time for yourself because other people in your life are "more important" or come first.

- Saying phrases like "must be nice" in reaction to people who are enjoying their lives or setting healthy boundaries.

When your sugar jar is below halfway full, you usually know it but are unsure about what to do about it. You might feel drained, tired, and overwhelmed, and still the to-do list appears to get longer.

The attributes of a life with a jar filled this way may include:

- Feeling overwhelmed and/or exhausted regularly.

- Saying yes without checking in with yourself first.

- Often feeling like no one cares about how much you have going on.

- Perhaps identifying as a "strong friend."

- Often feeling like you "have" to say yes because you are the best person to get it done.

- Perhaps having issues finishing projects because you really want everything to be done "right."

- Perhaps having issues receiving assistance or help from others.

- Perhaps feeling judgmental about people who take time off.

- Perhaps feeling that rest is like "being lazy."

You might be thinking, "Wait a minute, how am I going to keep my jar full? Isn't that a perfect life? Isn't that impossible? How will I live my life completely if all my time is focused on keeping my jar full?" Well, having a full jar means having enough spaciousness to have a fulfilling life, but your life doesn't have to be perfect to feel full. And that feeling of fullness comes when we decide to fill up our jars with our own sugar, not from the sugar of others, although people without lids on their jars or those who care about us may try, with love, to donate some of their sugar to us. But everyone has sugar that is completely unique to them.

Unless you are parenting, where we can give our sugar to our children, your sugar will be completely different from all the people you're in relationship with. Think of it as some people have granulated sugar, some people have raw sugar, and so on. If someone were to attempt to "give" you some of their sugar, it would never be the same as the sugar you have in your jar.

Have you ever dropped something in an actual jar of sugar in your home while cooking or getting tea or coffee? You might wrestle a spoon in to try to get the foreign object out of your jar, but somehow it seems to get more lost in all the sugar that belongs in the jar. This is also how it can feel when someone else's sugar is in your jar—yes, it helps to fill up space, but it doesn't belong there, and it can be hard to separate what's yours from what's theirs when it's mixed.

But can we also talk about how beautiful your sugar is? It's your laughter, your creativity, and your originality. Protecting your sugar is a priority so that you also get to enjoy it yourself. If you give all of it away, then at the end of the day, every day, you may feel like you have nothing to give to yourself. Protecting your sugar allows you to have space for all the exciting activities and experiences you look forward to. When you live your life where you are a priority, you're able to be there for those you love, dedicate yourself to the commitments you're interested in being a part of, and take care of yourself in a loving and attentive way.

YOUR LID

Your lid represents your boundaries, and when you take the lid off to expose your sugar, that act represents you giving permission to whatever has been asked of you. Your lid prevents your sugar from falling out, it prevents people from having access to your sugar without asking you, and it serves as a stopping point for you yourself. With the lid on your jar, you get a moment to ask yourself, before you take it off your jar, "Do I actually want to say yes to this?"

When you think about an actual jar of sugar, it has a lid on it. The lid helps keep the sugar fresh, it prevents things from getting into the sugar that you don't want in it, and it stops the sugar from being spilled out. The sugar jar is easier to manage with a lid on it.

Much like an actual jar of sugar, your sugar jar operates in the same way. Keeping a lid on your sugar jar is literally setting boundaries. It's also important to mention that you get to decide how open or closed your jar is and who has access to your jar whether open or closed. Perhaps your romantic partner has access to your jar with the lid off because of the comfort and trust you've built together. When you go to work, your jar might be closed, allowing you to open your jar only when you feel comfortable. Keeping the lid on your jar at all times isn't the goal, it's more about becoming familiar with why you open or close your jar, with whom you feel comfortable doing it, and ultimately how your choices are impacting you.

When you don't have boundaries in place, the lid is off your jar, with all of you being fully accessible and exposed for everyone in your life to have access to. People without lids on their jars may regularly feel overwhelmed, resentful, drained, and perhaps even used by the people in their lives. I'll mention again that your jar is your responsibility, which means that if people take your sugar without asking, it's because you don't have a lid on your jar, and that acts as you giving them permission to have access to you.

[NOTE: This, of course, is not applicable to people in abusive situations or relationships.]

You may also be wondering why when people see that your jar is without a lid, they take from it, when it feels as if they *should* know they shouldn't. Or perhaps if they see that the sugar in your jar is low, why would they just not ask? Unfortunately, that's often not how things work, because people rely on you to communicate to them how you're feeling and to explain what's okay and what's not okay. *When you don't share your boundaries, people may think that the absence of boundaries means yes.*

YOUR KITCHEN

Your sugar jar lives in your kitchen, which represents your life. And in real life, the kitchen is often the place where we connect, where we nourish ourselves, and where there's many moving parts—and it's no different from your energetic kitchen. All aspects of your relationships, your experiences, your career, your hobbies—everything resides in your kitchen. Ask yourself: Does my kitchen feel spacious or cluttered? Does my kitchen have a lot of light, or does it feel dreary? Does my kitchen need renovations? And if your kitchen needs renovations, do you find that you're often the one doing the renovations on your own or are you able to ask for help?

There are no right or wrong answers here, because you get to decide what feels good and aligned in your life. Your sugar jar should feel comfortable in your kitchen, not like an outsider. Sometimes we can feel like outsiders in our own lives, especially when we're living the life that others wanted for us or if we're consistently putting ourselves last.

For some, you may have a wonderful and expansive kitchen, but you feel called to keep your sugar jar in a cupboard or a pantry, hidden from view out of fear that people will want what they see. Get curious and ask yourself: What would it take for me to have my sugar jar living on a beautiful counter? What kinds of boundaries and structures would I need to put in place for me to feel comfortable living out loud in my kitchen without fear that the jar could be taken without my permission?

Your kitchen is the atmosphere around your sugar jar. It's where you have your tough conversations, where you do your entertaining, where your curl up to cry, and where others come to curl up and cry with you. This means that your kitchen is always evolving, with change being the only constant. This isn't to be feared, because the change taking place in your kitchen is what you allow. People can come in if you let them in. People can only take up space there if you let them. And, most likely, you take up space in other people's kitchens, too. At any time, you can decide to close your kitchen door for the moment and do a deep clean, light a candle, and just take it easy. You can decide to open the door and allow people to enjoy all the sweets available. There may also be times where the activities taking place in your kitchen feel out of your control and that's because life is often out of our control. In those moments, you still get to check in with yourself and decide what needs to shift to help you adapt to the current circumstances. You always get to choose how you adjust.

We all have a special relationship with our kitchen. Some of us are okay with leaving issues "in the sink overnight" while others like the kitchen to be as organized as possible before starting or ending their day. Some of us like our kitchen to be the one place where we don't have to do a bunch of adulting or chores, and so we prioritize rest by outsourcing many of the issues that come up in our kitchen via retreats, workshops, therapy, and coaches, while others feel comfortable with DIY via a great self-help book. No matter the relationship we have with our kitchen, none of us enjoy walking into our kitchen to find a mess that someone else has made. Having clear boundaries about who's allowed in and what's allowed in there can really help alleviate those issues.

JAR MAINTENANCE

Your sugar jar holds all of you, and so, of course, it may sometimes need maintenance work.

LEAKS

Sometimes, you may have someone in your life who's constantly asking you for time, attention, or resources that you don't actually want to give or perhaps you don't have the space to provide, and you might even feel guilty about not being able to meet their request. Perhaps you don't feel guilty, but you want to keep the peace, so you don't enforce your boundaries the way you should. In those cases, you might be thinking, "I've put my lid on (aka boundaries), but I still feel extremely depleted, why is that?" Sometimes, even with the lid on, your jar can have a leak, where the sugar is seeping out of an area that has a crack or splice in it. It may be just a little bit of sugar at a time, almost unnoticeable. But those little leaks can add up.

Leaks usually show up in relationships or situations where you've already set the boundary (aka you've put the lid on your jar), but they're still behaving like the boundary isn't there and you aren't stopping them. Instead of tampering with the lid, they look around your jar for another way in, a crack or an opening where the sugar is leaking. Why would you have a sugar leak? Sometimes, we go against our own boundaries, and it's not only by saying yes when we mean no, but by not saying or doing anything when a boundary we've put in place is being violated. The boundary still exists, but it isn't being enforced.

This is an important distinction because sometimes we think, "I've put the boundary in place, why is this still happening?" And there may be many answers to this question. Are you afraid to have a tough conversation and address the boundary violation? Are you nervous about a potential confrontation, so you ignore the boundary violation? Is there a part of you that thinks that your boundary is "over the top," and therefore even though the boundary is in place, you feel guilty about enforcing it? Leaks always occur when we ignore our boundaries and allow behaviors or circumstances to happen without advocating for ourselves. People don't have to take your lid off to access you. They can also look for cracks in your beliefs about your boundaries or your jar that allow them in.

UPSIZE/DOWNSIZE

There may be times where you'll feel like you need a bigger jar to hold more capacity for the changes happening in your life. Maybe you've just decided to have children, or perhaps you're birthing a creative project. In the same way, there are occasions where you may notice that a smaller jar would better suit your current circumstances. Maybe you've just left a career and you've decided to slow down for a bit with gentle travel. Or perhaps you realized that the way you were living your life felt a bit overwhelming to keep up with, so you've changed the number of events that you say yes to or how much you travel so that you don't need as much space for sugar.

The important thing to know is that you are capable and have full autonomy to change your jar size anytime you feel called to. What someone else considers large, you might consider small and vice versa. What someone else considers tough to manage may feel just right to you.

SUGAR SIFTING

Earlier we talked about how sometimes a foreign object, like coffee or tea, can get into actual sugar jars and it can be tough to get it out, right? And sometimes, by accident, while grabbing some real-life sugar with a spoon for our coffee or tea, the spoon might be a bit wet, and so it causes clumps of sugar to form. We've all seen this, too, right?

In the same way that this happens in an actual sugar jar, this can also happen in your metaphorical sugar jar. Even with the best boundaries, there may be times when someone else's energy or other substance ends up in your jar. Sometimes you may not be able to clearly discern what's there, but you can sense that you feel a bit "off" after a disagreement or even a fun but hectic week of traveling. In those cases, you can begin to sift your sugar to see what can help you release any of the foreign objects or energy that got into your jar that doesn't belong there.

And as for the clumps or lumps of sugar that may be present in your jar, you may want to "break" them up because they inhibit the flow of sugar in your jar that should be there. Sometimes they can also make you think your jar is full when, if that clump was broken down, you'd find that there's not as much sugar as it seems.

FILLING YOUR JAR

This is where all the self-care and wellness tools become the main character. Taking care of yourself is how you either fill your sugar jar or keep your jar full of the sugar that's already there. As you begin to check in with yourself, you'll learn what works best for your jar.

For example, for one person having a one-hour phone conversation with a friend might feel invigorating and they end the conversation with one cup of sugar added to their jar. For another person, that same conversation might leave them feeling depleted and exhausted, even if it was a friendly conversation, and now they need to do something to fill their jar back up.

Things don't have to be negative to deplete your jar. Some things just require more energy from you than others. Everyone is different and each sugar jar will have its own recipes. Below are some examples so that you can get a better idea of how the measurements of filling your jar might work:

- A 15-minute meditation might add ½ cup of sugar.

- A 30-minute walk might add 1 cup of sugar.

- 6 to 8 hours of restful sleep might add 2 cups of sugar.

- A funny movie might add ½ cup of sugar.

- A canceled plan that didn't feel right might retain 2 to 3 cups of sugar.

- An unanswered phone call from someone who's harmful might retain 2 to 3 cups of sugar.

- A therapy or coaching session might add 2 cups of sugar.

- A period of time (decided by you) completely devoted to your wellness might fill your jar.

P.S. You don't have to know how many cups of sugar your jar can hold. Since you oversee how big or small your jar is, the true "depth" of your jar is infinite. The measurements just help with understanding how something could be adding or taking away from your sugar jar. And even when you say yes to things that end up being drains, remember that you may "lose" sugar temporarily, but you can always add it back by taking care of yourself.

SUGAR JAR CHECK-IN

- What kind of jar do you have?

- What kind of jar would you like?

- What's keeping you from changing it?

- Do you want a different-size jar?

- Would you like a different type of sugar or texture?

- Would you like a spoon for your jar so that when your energy is used, it is dispersed with more specificity?

- Would you like a different kind of lid for your jar?

- What did you learn about your energy?

- What felt good about the space where your jar lives?

- Is there anything you'd like to change before we go any further?

Say It with Me

This journey may be messy, but this doesn't mean I'm doing anything wrong.

I have full permission to change my mind at any time.

2

BLACK HEALING

NOTE: Although this book is for everyone, I dedicate this chapter to Black healing and what we often navigate through because of harmful societal norms, racism, and ignorance. I speak from my Black experience and culture as well as my experience as a facilitator. I realized that I have rarely, if ever, read a book by a non-Black wellness or healing writer that has centered on Black people and our desire for healing. When I have seen our experiences mentioned, it usually relies heavily on our trauma and pain being centered. Although I share some of the collective Black American experience here, if you're non-Black this is not necessarily the experience of every Black American, and it's still always important to listen and learn.

I hope that this chapter is an invitation for Black people to look at yourselves as humans literally being in this world with hopes, dreams, and desires beyond the stories of our suffering. This chapter is not intended to be a teaching tool for anyone who isn't Black. If you identify as a person of color, I do believe that some of this chapter may resonate with you, too.

I was attending a wellness course and we were in the last couple of weeks before it ended. During that week, there were a lot of news stories and blog posts highlighting the uptick in racist behavior and commentary and how it was translating into real-life violence. I felt angry, frightened, and overwhelmed, so I went into the online group to post about my experiences and share my fears. We were regularly encouraged to post in the online group when feelings were coming up and I'd done this so many other times about every other topic, like money, feminism, or relationships, but this was my first time talking about race with the group. Usually, when you post in the group, other women will support you, share their thoughts, help you find alternatives, and ultimately be there with you as you coped. But this time, unbeknownst to me, I'd lit a fire in that group.

As the comments rolled in on my post, I sat there in tears. Women who had openly presented themselves as "woke" were clearly not doing the work that being woke entails. Before I knew it, I was debating my feelings and my experiences, and arguing with the group. And what's interesting is that I never mentioned or called out anyone specifically in the group in my initial post, but their responses were the words of people who felt that I had uncovered something about them that they didn't want unearthed. As my grandmother used to say, "A hit dog will holler."

Finally, the facilitator of the group joined the conversation. Naively, I was waiting for her to come in and help the non-Black women, who were feeling personally attacked by me sharing my feelings, understand that they had personal work to do. But instead, she invited us to a call where she'd share more on the topic, and on that call she openly told me, in front of the group, that if I wanted to talk about my experiences as a Black woman as it pertains to racism that I should "create my own community elsewhere." She wanted me to be silent, and she made it clear to everyone else that she thought their behavior toward me was completely okay. She followed this up with "We're all human and when you choose to think otherwise, by dividing us based on color, we're missing the point. Go deeper and figure out why color is becoming such a block for you."

I was so completely caught off guard. I proceeded to go off in that online group since I didn't have the opportunity to be unmuted on the call. But truly, I was deeply embarrassed. I couldn't believe I had invested in a program like that. How did I miss the signs? I felt alone and foolish. Out of almost one-hundred-plus women in the group who were witnessing this, only two supported me. And even though there were weeks left of the program, which I had paid thousands to attend, I decided to leave early as I knew

that I had reached my limit and would not feel comfortable continuing to learn from someone who felt this way. It wasn't the
first experience where I'd had a non-Black or white person try to
silence me, but it was the first one that was so blatant. For her to
feel at ease, I would have to play small and hide my reality for her
comfort. And even though this was the exact opposite of what
she was teaching, when it came to confronting racism, that was a
step too far for her. I have seen this happen in so many wellness
communities where there isn't true accountability and diversity as
it's claimed.

As a Black woman, I've always wanted the opportunity to move
freely through the world being as soft as I choose, as vulnerable
as I choose, and as fluid as I choose to be. Not feeling any need to
do or be anything other than who I am. Not having to fit into any
particular box that I don't feel I belong in. Not having to offer myself up for consumption to anyone. The reality is that I've had to
be very intentional about creating space for myself to have access
to that gentle energy as it's not what I was taught was available to
me. And the other reality is that it's a struggle to let the gentleness
in, even when I know I'm deserving of it.

As humans, we all have our experiences, traumas, pain, suffering, and circumstances to process. But as Black humans, we
come encoded with the heaviness of those before us as well as a
sense, from as early as we can tap into the consciousness of our
world, that we're carrying a heavy weight in the present. Naturally,
when someone discovers a bruise, they try to figure out how they
can heal it. But when you're Black, it's tough to learn that our

inherited bruises, our bruises from society and culture, and our bruises from our lived experiences aren't always welcomed or understood. There's a belief that our ability to endure pain is endless, and sometimes we accept that belief as truth, forgetting ourselves in the process. Our strength is often used against us because we don't often receive other options. Unless we get the opportunity to be invited into softness early on in our lives, many of us don't know it's available until well into our adult years or, worse, we never feel safe enough to try it.

Sometimes, there's an inherited fear of vulnerability because we're aware of the responsibility we own in creating safety in our world in a way that's very different from non-Black people. Black healing in non-Black or white spaces often focuses on all that we've lost and centers around us continuing to share our trauma, and that sharing can sometimes become an educational opportunity for others where debate eclipses understanding, which is harmful. The focus should always be on learning how to have moments where we feel safe enough to put down our armor and be our freest, most joyful, whole selves. No apology. Full stop.

We don't heal differently, but we often need different things. We require a safe space to be held for us that is culturally supportive of who we are, what we've been through, what our parents or those who raised us have endured, and what our ancestors were forced to live through. We require this amid a society that ignores our history, which we internally and through community work to rectify. We need a space where we don't have to explain why it's hard to hold everything that we're living through in this moment.

When I was growing up, I spent a lot of time with my grand-mother, who was born in the early 1920s in the South. She was raised by my great-great-grandmother, who was born a slave and later sharecropped with her husband. I can vividly recall my grandmother's stories of what it was like sharecropping in South Carolina, where she would sneak a taste of the cream that would form on top of the milk that was in the barrels. I remember hear-ing stories of how they'd smoke meat for the winter. I remember hearing how hard it was for them when the Great Depression hit. And I remember how much her world changed when she, among millions of other African Americans, made the great migration north, and she chose Harlem, New York, to meet her mother, my great-grandmother, who was already there. I always found it fasci-nating that my life was being infused by the experiences of people who had lived through a time that society tried to teach us was something that happened "a long time ago." But here my grand-mother and great-grandmother were, right in front of me, living examples that I was being brought up through their strength and perseverance during times that were still very current.

If you asked me about something that I remembered doing with both my grandmother and great-grandmother regularly, it was watching *Jeopardy!* or *Wheel of Fortune* each evening. My grandmother would ask me to go over to the TV and adjust the antenna, making sure the picture was as crisp as it could be as we settled in to fully participate in the game-show activities. We might've been at home, but we were contestants on those shows as far as we were concerned. Every now and then someone would yell out an answer in the room and then we'd discuss what we thought would happen and who we believed would win. The magic of those nights was always heightened when the guests were being introduced and one of them was Black. There was an energy in the room like we knew that person. And it's because in many ways, we did know that person. Although we're all different, we felt we connected. We didn't have to know anything about them to also know so much about them. An entire history of conversations shared without having ever said a word.

If they got an answer right, we shouted with joy and excitement. If they lost money that round, we were shouting "That's okay, you've still got this! Come on!" And if they happened to win the game show, well, we'd all celebrate as if we all were about to cash the check as well. We understood that when Black people won it created space and opportunity for all of us. And because we got to witness their win, it was even better, because now that we'd seen it, we could believe it was possible for us. I like to think about this when I think about Black healing as well. The more we normalize seeing Black people living lives that aren't grounded in pain but instead filled with light, the more we can see how it's possible for all of us. It doesn't mean there won't be ups and downs. It doesn't mean we won't face difficulties. But we can access jubilation.

It's a reminder that many things can be true about our experiences. If my choice to heal can soothe wounds within my lineage, then I can also reach back and access the strength of my lineage, the light of my lineage, and the guidance of my lineage. If my ancestors dance at the sound of intergenerational trauma cords breaking, then I also have access to the new vows of abundance being curated on my behalf. The beauty of duality is that we're not just holding the tough parts. We give ourselves the freedom to recognize all that we can access while resisting anything that no longer fits. Our story is our story. Where we come from is where we come from. Neither has any bearing on who we can become or what we can create.

But sometimes, healing can feel tough when we know that many of the systems that we live in try to keep us small. In much of the wellness rhetoric, we're taught to generally "manifest" our way out of our circumstances. It's often one of the first things people come across in healing work, and it usually feels like a super-powerful and exciting tool. And to be clear, manifestation is an amazing tool that can help all of us begin to bring our desires into fruition, especially when we combine manifestation with action. But the way manifestation is normally taught often ignores the work that's involved to bring dreams to reality, it often ignores the access to information that's required to get started, and it often ignores the privilege that's necessary to automatically uproot your life.

Manifestation is often taught without the perspective or recognition of the real-life roadblocks Black people experience, and to be clear this doesn't mean we don't belong in all of these spaces—we do. But the idea that "if you think it, it will be" excludes the validated experiences of racism, redlining, race and gender wage gaps, oppression, and so much more. Even if we just focus on the inequality in the wellness and healing community, we can see the disproportion in access for Black people. Does this mean that Black people can't create lives that match their manifestations? Absolutely not and thank goodness that's not true. But the reality is that there are systems in place that may require a lot more from us than it may for non-Black people or non-Black people of color based on the unconscious bias, stereotypes, and racism that exists in all spaces.

I don't share this so that you feel limited in what you can accomplish, but instead I hope it empowers you to find a way to create your idea of abundance in your life no matter what. When we validate our truths and acknowledge our reality, we're able to make way for new possibilities and advocate for change. We can still experience the magic of manifestation while acknowledging how our path might be different than what others experience.

Healing looks different when:

- You sign up for a wellness or healing retreat and find you're one of two Black people in the room.

- You have trouble finding a therapist in your area who looks like you or understands your culture.

- You have to do extra research to ensure that your vacation destination, which was booked with restoration in mind, is safe for Black people.

- You find that walking home, running in your neighborhood, driving, or even sleeping in your bed can be a dangerous place to be.

- You know that your experiences aren't validated by the world.

- You find that the educational institutions that are supposed to inform you uphold oppressive stances and share inaccurate history.

- You're told not to "make it about race" when literally everything you do ends up involving it anyway.

I share this perspective on manifestation because even in my experience in that wellness course I mentioned above, I became brutally aware of how although I was welcomed to pay for healing experiences and wellness education, I could not expect the coursework or the conversation to reflect my reality, no matter how diverse and welcoming they were attempting to market themselves as. I was hoping wellness would be the place where racial bias couldn't exist. I was incredibly wrong, and for a long time I carried a lot of shame about finally feeling ready to step into my healing journey and then being met with so much racism. It's this very experience that catapulted me fully into facilitating healing work, recognizing that I could be a part of the solution by holding healthful space for all healing, but especially for Black healing.

I'm not attempting to speak for every Black person's experience and I understand that grouping our experiences together is often something that happens which doesn't leave space for all of the different ways we show up to be explored. I hope this conversation opens an internal dialogue about how you can take care of yourself without attempting to fit into the societal boxes that weren't made for us. Of course, we can't change everything and everyone around us alone, and it would be draining to try. But when it comes to Black healing, we can be intentional about our joy. We can be intentional about our peace. And we can create a life that reflects the light within us.

TOXIC POSITIVITY +
SPIRITUAL BYPASSING

If I was asked to name something that's incredibly harmful to a Black person who is healing it would be toxic positivity and spiritual bypassing. And to be clear, toxic positivity and spiritual bypassing are often fueled by racism. Let me explain.

In wellness, there's sometimes this incredible push to completely focus on the positive and on good things, and it's encouraged that doing this can accelerate our healing. Think "love and light." Now, there's absolutely nothing wrong with love and there's nothing wrong with light, but it is not the answer to everything. And to get to the place where we can fully experience "love and light" we're encouraged to address what's blocking them, and this will be different for every individual person. When "love and light" becomes the answer, we're often being asked to ignore our discomfort and instead invited to "try to focus on the positive." I have seen how this can be more prevalent when Black people bring up their culturally specific experiences and we're asked to "stop focusing on the past," to "stop sounding so angry," when sharing our frustrations and worries, and we may even have non-Black people share with us that they "don't see color" as an uninformed way of trying to connect.

Toxic positivity is harmful. It completely undermines your experiences and can cause feelings of shame or guilt because after you've bravely shared your truth, toxic positivity rejects it. The reality is that there needs to be space for what's tough but true for you to be heard so that you can infuse your life with what feels like love and light for you, not based on what others define them as being.

It's important to understand when this is happening to you so that you can identify it and address it by either advocating for what you need, setting a boundary, or perhaps finding someone else to hold space for you. **Sometimes when your truth triggers others, their response is to try to create a reality where your truth doesn't exist instead of doing the work**

of exploring why they're triggered in the first place. And in creating a reality where you and your truth don't exist, they attempt to eliminate you and your experiences from real life and instead proceed to try to push the fantasy that's probably more comfortable for them.

Spiritual bypassing is just as rampant in wellness and uses many of the same "love and light" or "good vibes only" language from toxic positivity, but it goes a step further by completely erasing the experiences of Black people and people of color while using spirituality as the disguise. In the wellness course that I mentioned above, their entire existence was built on visiting the shadow, aka the tough stuff, to bring the light forward. It blew my mind that this space was promoting wellness, but racism was often seen as a distraction from doing what they considered to be "the real work" rather than an opportunity to truly dive in.

Spiritual bypassing and toxic positivity don't only show up in wellness and healing communities, they show up at school, at work, in friend groups, and anywhere that there are people who don't fully understand the reality that Black people and people of color live in. If you're showing up in a space to receive healing, then you shouldn't also be responsible for teaching those attending with you or the facilitators about their unconscious bias, but I have seen this happen so many times.

These experiences cause leaks in your sugar jar. It's not your job to disrupt every single space you walk into and use all your energy to educate others. You might feel like it's a part of your work to explain, share, and teach others to help make the world

a better place. And there's nothing wrong with being an advocate or educator; thank goodness for those who take on this
heavy task. But even advocates deserve time where they're just
being nourished and taken care of. And so do you! You deserve
time where you're able to take off the heavy weight and feel the
freedom that comes with it. You deserve time where you aren't
teaching anyone anything about your experience, and instead
you're able to just live in it, finding the peace as you journey.
You deserve to be heard and understood just as you are, no
debate.

PRIORITIZING YOUR SUGAR JAR

There are so many potential energy drains throughout our day
and learning how to protect our sugar is important because it
ensures that we have enough to pour into ourselves.

Ask yourself: What consistent drains do I have in my life that I
want to remove? What keeps me from removing them?

How can I create space and time where I'm okay with giving
attention to tough issues, but also create space and time where
those issues are off limits?

When is my sugar and my jar just about me?

It's tough, but a big part of ensuring that you protect your sugar
will be ensuring that you're not constantly being bombarded with
everything that's going on around you. Being informed is very
different than being consumed. And while it's important to stay

aware, it's okay and important to honor that you need to have times where you're not holding it all.

ASK YOURSELF:

- Where does the light come from in my life?

- Where do I feel safest in my life?

- Whom am I with when I feel I can completely be myself?

- What do I need and how can I give it to myself? Or, how can I ask for help?

When answering these questions, I want you to think about how you can make space in your life to experience as much of the joy and ease as you do everything else. It won't always be easy but it's worth it because if we want a life that offers us joy and peace we have to go after it and make it happen. We must be willing to bring it into our lives.

It's also important to ask yourself how some of the limiting beliefs you carry got into you. These beliefs can cause our sugar to form into lumps, limiting the flow of sugar within our jar. This doesn't mean you've done anything wrong, as we all inherit "lumps of sugar" from our families, experiences, friends, and tough times. It's just an invitation for you to bring some flow back into your jar.

ASK YOURSELF:

- Are these limiting beliefs mine or were they passed down to me?

- Did I experience this pain, or did I inherit it through my lineage?

- Is the fear that I feel coming from my experiences?

Whether these beliefs are inherited or gained through your own experiences, you can begin to ask yourself what you might need to rewrite these stories, gently walking yourself through the process of making a different choice. For example, if you're afraid that a particular goal may not be possible for you because you're unsure of how to make it happen, think about other times in your life where you were unsure of how you'd make something happen and how you were eventually able to find the resources you needed to follow through. And sometimes just giving yourself the freedom to vent about how hard something feels is helpful in moving energy, reducing those lumps in our sugar jar, and making space for flow and ease again.

PRACTICE CONSTRUCTIVE COMPLAINING

So often we feel like we have to keep all our emotions in and that's draining. When we hold in our pain, discomfort, and fears, it's like taking a chisel to our jar and creating a leak for our sugar to seep right out of. Constructive complaining gives us permission to be honest about what's hard, what sucks, what we feel, what we wish we didn't have to feel—anything that's coming up. Complaining gets a bad rap, especially in our culture, and sometimes we just need to let it all out. Remind yourself that constructive complaining is self-care.

Grab your journal, grab a friend, or open the voice notes section of your phone and let. it. out. If you choose a friend, let them know what you need them to hold space for so that they can assess their jars and ensure they can show up for you! For example, you'd ask, "Hey, do you have space to hear some constructive complaining? I need some support."

YOU DESERVE TO HEAL

We tend to feel so much responsibility for not only ourselves but our family, our community, and the collective community that we're a part of. And with good reason because we know the power of unification and we understand the importance of providing accessibility and information. Being an important member of your family unit, community, or collective community still doesn't absolve you of needing support, too. While taking care of and supporting those around you, you can still work to support yourself. You **still** deserve to heal and be well.

From as early as I can remember, I was taught the importance of having to work incredibly hard if I wanted to stand out. We all know the "you've got to be ten times better" phrase. Not only because I'm a woman, but because I'm a Black woman. This resilience taught me to have an incredible work ethic and a discipline that I still carry with me throughout everything that I do. But that resilience burned me out because I didn't know how to turn that part of me off. Now that I've brought wellness into my life, I can apply that same resilience and discipline that I used in every other area of my life toward my healing. I can support myself, take care of myself, and advocate for my healing. I can stand up for myself, with others and sometimes with myself, by reminding myself that I matter, too.

In Dr. Maya Angelou's interview with Oprah Winfrey on *Super Soul Sunday* she shares:

> *You've been paid for by people who never even saw your face. Your mother's mother, your father's father. And so it behooves you to prepare yourself so you can pay for someone else yet to come. Whose name you'll never know. You just keep the good thing going.*

I carry this with me as a reminder that I'm supported, even when I didn't see it. It's a reminder that it's okay to follow the call to care for myself. And that when I do this, I'm encouraging and inviting others to do the same. And I'm filling my jar for the times when I'll need to be there for others.

TAKE UP SPACE

You don't have to apologize for being who you are. Ever. The thought of living unapologetically can feel enticing but difficult.

Choosing to be and taking up space in a world that wasn't built for us is brave because we're committing to doing the very opposite of what society normalizes we should do.

ASK YOURSELF:

- What would I do if I wasn't afraid of what anyone else would think?

- How would I live my life if I was primarily concerned with what fulfilled me first?

- How can I learn to not allow other people's discomfort to stop me?

- What does "taking up space" look like in my life?

Here are some examples of the ways you can take up space:

- Making decisions that align with your desires, even if they're not the norm.

- Using the *S* from the S.U.G.A.R. acronym and saying no. Boundaries give you more space for you.

- Advocating for what you need (e.g., asking for pay commensurate with your experience).

- Bringing your culture with you wherever you go.

- Celebrating your achievements.

- Remembering that there's enough room for you to be at the table, too. And if not, a new table can always be obtained or created.

BE CLEAR ON WHAT YOU NEED,
LEAVE THE REST

Your power lies in your ability to consistently question what really needs to take up space in your life and to release everything that doesn't. This means that you don't have to exist in the world in any way other than exactly as you want to. There's power in ensuring that you don't forget yourself in the decisions you make. Life can be distracting when we're taught that assimilation or "fitting in" is the only way to make it, within your culture or outside of it. Standing firmly in your knowing is an important way to choose you.

It's also important to be clear on how you will continue to stay informed on important Black issues without losing yourself in the process. For example, I've personally made the choice to not watch any videos of violence against Black people. I stay informed while also being careful of how much I ingest, because I've noticed that I'm not able to be present in my role, as a space holder and healer for others, when I immerse myself in watching those horrible acts. I'm not able to be there for myself or my children when I tune in to those videos. I've learned that I can advocate and say their names without perpetuating the unhealthy voyeurism cycle of Black pain and grief. I take in what I need to know so that I can advocate, and I leave the rest. I've learned that we fight our best fights when our sugar jars are full, and that's what we don't often get to do. Live in our fullness.

THE EASE

ASK YOURSELF:

- What does gentleness look like to me?

- How do I allow myself to be soft?

- How do I allow my life to have ease in it and throughout it?

Committing to a life that requires less doing and more ease doesn't mean you'll be "lazy," and it also doesn't mean it won't require intentional planning. But it may require you to discard beliefs that prevent you from envisioning and thus living a life that is fueled by peace and joy. This is where the magic of manifestation, visualization, and ease can really come in.

Ask yourself: If I'm going to commit to working hard, what would it feel like to work hard for the reality I desire? What would it feel like to let go of the parts of my reality that keep me in unhealthy cycles? What would it feel like to live with joy as a major part of my life?

Say It with Me

I release any beliefs that limit my growth.

I'm allowed ease and I can create a life that mirrors all that I desire.

My needs are greater than their comfort.

3

PRESENCE OVER PERFORMANCE

Several years ago, I wanted to learn more about the inner workings of business, so I attended an in-person business workshop that was included in the price of an online course I'd purchased. I was incredibly excited to attend this event to learn, network, and meet new people, something I was inviting myself to do at the time. Even though I'd interacted with some of the course members online, this would be our first time actually meeting in person. As an introvert, I'm more comfortable at home, but I wanted to try to get out of my comfort zone.

I was incredibly nervous about this event because it took place on the Upper East Side of Manhattan, in New York City. It was my first real time in this area, even though I was born and raised in Brooklyn and have spent time in all five boroughs through my childhood and adult life. But there wasn't a circumstance that would've brought me to the Upper East Side up until that point because it wasn't where my friends or family lived, shopped, or spent time.

Now if you're not from New York City or you've never visited this area, it's incredibly opulent. The sidewalks literally sparkle, almost completely absent of the large black spots of old gum that usually show up on city streets. There are doormen at every entrance of every residential building wearing uniforms emblazoned with gold buttons and white gloves, opening the doors as people come and go. In the morning, workers are washing the sidewalks. There is barely any trash on the streets, a rarity in New York. And unlike anywhere else in the city, it is quiet in the morning. It's not suburban quiet, but it's quiet. It encompasses Fifth Avenue, Park Avenue, and Madison Avenue and is known as the home neighborhood of some of the wealthiest people. And early that morning, when I was heading to this event, walking down the pretty deserted streets, I felt out of place in my hometown for the first time ever.

As I got closer to the event space, impostor syndrome became even louder. I asked myself, *What am I doing here? Why did I ever imagine that I would "fit in" with the people who would be here? And what will they think of me?*

When I walked into the beautiful town house, I was greeted by a chic host with a big smile, who gave me a name tag and showed me where the breakfast table was. I walked across the intimate red and gold room to my seat, which was by the floor-to-ceiling windows, and smiled politely at those who smiled at me as I took in the room. As I sat among the women there, I saw that every single one of them had on multiple Cartier bracelets, there were a few Hermès bags that I'd honestly never seen in person before, and it appeared that many of the women had met before as they were chatting away about dinners at this location or taking their kids to the park at that location. It was a different language than my own.

I want you to understand that I have nothing against designer clothing, I love it, in fact. There was a part of me that was excited to see all this glitz and glam. But it's also important to paint the picture of how I began to capture evidence based on how others were living their lives as proof that I didn't belong there and it was quickly morphing into "I don't belong here and I'm not worthy of being here." This was before I even got to know anyone. This was before the event officially started. I chose this event because I knew it would be a different group of people than I was used to being around, but I didn't realize how the environment would affect my feeling of belonging. Sometimes we believe that because we don't have access to certain things that other people do it means we don't belong, and that's so far from the truth. But on this day, I didn't know that yet.

Once the event began, I quickly recognized that the content was more advanced than I was ready for in my business. That didn't mean that I wouldn't be able to take away things from the event, because I did learn a lot, but all of this didn't help my impostor-syndrome feelings. And what I didn't realize at the time was that I was at an event for people who were much further along in business than I was, as evidenced by the questions they asked about scaling and building teams. I had never felt so out of place.

Instead of sharing any discomfort, with myself or anyone else, I pushed my cute-as-hell Zara bag under the table, and I pushed my feelings there, too. One thing I knew how to do was pretend that I was okay even if I wasn't. I was going to *pretend* I was enjoying myself even though I wanted to run out of there during our lunch break of perfectly crust-cut sandwiches, grab a hero (NYC slang for a sub), and never return.

As far as I was concerned, everyone else was thinking the exact negative thoughts about me that I was thinking about myself. It was in this very moment that I knew I had a choice. The host was talking and was about to ask everyone at the tables to do self-introductions. What would I tell them? How would I relate? How could I make it through this eight-hour workshop with people who appeared to be miles ahead of me?

BELONGING

Have you noticed how much of what I shared and what I remembered from the event were conversations that were occurring in my own head, with myself? I didn't share any conversations or interactions with anyone that prompted me to believe that I didn't belong; in fact, no one said that I didn't belong. There were a couple of people who were a bit standoffish, but that's to be expected in any group.

- I had already decided that I didn't believe I belonged there before I even walked into the event.

- I decided that I didn't belong based on my background and what I'd been programmed to believe about people who are from where I'm from.

- I decided that I didn't belong based on my financial status.

- I decided that I didn't belong based on the external material things that they had that I couldn't afford at the time.

It's also important to mention that part of my story was valid. Class **does** exist and does exclude people. The potential for someone to think that I shouldn't be at an event for businesses in the expansion stage when I was still in the start-up phase was also **likely**. But despite these points, **it never meant that I wasn't worthy**. It never meant that I didn't belong to myself. It never meant that I'd be better as someone else.

And because I didn't want them to know what I thought was true about myself, which was that I was an impostor and didn't belong in that room, I chose to perform. I laughed when they laughed. I behaved like I related to their stories when I really didn't. I said I might be at events with them later on that year when I truly had no idea what they were talking about. I put on a show, for them, but really for myself. I was so embarrassed.

As the event ended, the attendee who was sitting next to me asked with a smile, "Did you take it all in today?" "Yup, I learned a lot today that I'm excited to take back home with me," I answered while packing up. And it was true, I did learn a lot that day. But I also tore myself apart inside the entire time. I missed the opportunity to ask the real questions that I had because for some reason being a beginner or not knowing the answers was translating internally that I was a failure. And even if it was true, that I had failed at a particular project or an idea at some point, I was still learning. It was all a lesson. But again I didn't have those tools in my kitchen yet. So instead I left with a drained and depleted sugar jar because I chose to show up as who I thought I needed to be rather than showing up as who I really was. Instead of staying in my beloved city that night, I got straight on the E train to head to Penn Station and got the hell out of there.

PERFORMING ISN'T ALWAYS
ABOUT DECEIT

Performing drains our sugar emotionally, physically, mentally, and spiritually. Why? Because every time we say yes to performing, we're also saying "Yes, I believe that who I am isn't enough" or "Yes, I'll show up as this person because showing up as I am won't work." Performing is acting because it's the real-life expression of the internal belief that we're not enough as we are, so the only option is to be someone else to belong.

I don't know about you, but when I was growing up, whenever we had company coming over to our house, we always had to clean it like there was going to be an inspection. No dishes could be in the sink, everything had to be double dusted, and anything out of place had to be put in its place. It was an all-hands-on-deck event. Now there's nothing wrong with having a clean home before guests come over, in fact, it's polite, but I always thought it was funny that it appeared as if that was the way we operated all the time. No one's house is completely spotless 24/7. Even though our home was already clean, we always knew the stressful deep cleaning was coming before guests arrived. Sometimes we do this very same thing in our kitchens, quickly sweeping any sugar under the rug before people walk into our lives so that they don't see that we're struggling to keep our sugar jars together.

Performing is often happening without our conscious permission. So many of us auto-perform before we even have the chance to realize that we're doing it. Much of the programming we received from our families, friends, and experiences fuels our programming to perform. People who attend this type of event should have *this* and I don't, so I need to act like I do. People who go on dates with someone who looks like this should have *this* and I don't, so I'll perform like I do. People who hang out with friends like this should have *this* and I don't, so I need to pretend that I do.

You're probably not performing because you necessarily want to lie or deceive others. In the story I shared above, I performed with the belief that it would make things "easier" because I thought being a beginner would be a burden. We also perform to fit in, to keep others happy, or to keep the peace. Performing also happens so that you conform to the world around you, as so many of us have been taught to do. Much of what society considers to be professional behavior, or how we should behave, is based on biased and unhealthy standards that don't fully account for our individual needs, feelings, or beliefs. Many of us choose to stay silent about who we are in order to fit in.

Performing is so ingrained in every part of society that it is taught and passed down as the norm. It is taught and passed down even though it hurts in the hope that the next generation will also "belong." But if we're all performing, then the gag is that few of us belong to anything except the standards we're trying to uphold.

"CASUAL" PERFORMING

Most of us have performed or pretended that everything was okay when it really wasn't. I call this "casual" performing because we've programmed ourselves to believe that it's okay to push our feelings to the side so that we'll be seen as strong or professional or to not burden others. And, of course, there are times and circumstances where you may consciously choose not to share your true emotions because it's not the right time or person. But too often the default is to not share at all and to pretend. And for many of you, you may have received the message early on that it's best to pretend because it hurts more when others don't show empathy or compassion for what you're going through.

Performance takes you out of your self-awareness. Instead of asking yourself, "Does this feel right to me?" you might be asking yourself something like "Will this feel right to them?" Presence ensures that you decipher what feels right to you before you accept anything from anyone. Without presence it's hard to set boundaries. Without presence it's hard to know what feels true to you. Without presence you can live your whole life doing what others think is best for you, or what you think others want from you, rather than living in your truth.

It's also important to know that you might think that the way you show up when you're pretending is who you really are. You may feel this way because you saw other family members with the same behavior, and like a family recipe, generation after generation, the instructions on how to handle your sugar jar were passed down to every member of the family nervous to adjust it, even if changing the recipe would better meet their needs.

PUSHING THROUGH

Sometimes we get so used to performing that we start to believe that being able to push ourselves past what feels good is a sign of strength or resilience. This type of performance enables us to pretend that we're comfortable when we're not. We pretend we have more time when we don't. We pretend we're well rested when we're drained. We pretend we're excited to commit to something when we'd rather not be a part of it.

Sometimes we push through because we don't want to hurt others. Sometimes we push through because we hope or have been taught that "it'll make us stronger." Sometimes we push through because we think it's too late to change our minds. Pushing through something that is tough, like training for the Olympics, because you want to do it and it's a real desire of yours is different than pushing yourself to take on extra projects at work, without pay, when you don't want to do them, but you're nervous to share how you really feel because you feel you *should* be doing it if they asked you to.

Pushing through usually happens when we don't have strong boundaries, and if we decide to push through and we make it, we might start believing that we *can* handle what's actually overwhelming us and so therefore boundaries alone isn't the answer. It's important to remind ourselves that surviving pushing through is not the same as thriving. Unlearning the desire to pretend that all is well when it isn't is a crucial part of being present to what you need versus performing.

SOME MORE WAYS THAT WE PERFORM

- Making decisions in our relationships based on what we wish the relationship was instead of accepting what it is.

- Staying in unhealthy or toxic relationships with the hope that the person will eventually change based on the "good" we see in them.

- Ignoring red flags.

- Not speaking up when something doesn't feel good.

- Choosing the ideology of being the bigger person over saying how we really feel.

- Believing in the notion that we're stronger than others and can therefore push through situations, experiences, and relationships that are hurting us.

"IT'S WHAT GOOD PEOPLE DO"

If you were taught to believe that being there for people no matter what is what "good" people do, then you most likely try your best to follow through and "be good." Most of you can probably remember that from the time you could do anything on your own, you've had your "goodness" thrown at you as a possible badge of honor and a key to being accepted in the world. Over time, many of us believe that this perceived goodness is literally how you access love and affection in the world. It's often externally validated by the relationships that we participate in. You show up and do the thing that you've been taught people expect of you and then the people you do it for are happy. You might believe this is what your worth is built on. And so you do everything in your power to receive that reaction from others over and over again without knowing that it isn't a true representation of what you want or who you are. Not that you don't enjoy helping people or making them happy. But if that's a large part of what you identify yourself to be, you might be pushing through to honor your commitment to "goodness." For example, if you've said, "My [insert here] (friends, family, coworkers, etc.) love that I'm always there for them no matter what." That "no matter what" part should always be investigated! I'm there for them "no matter what" meaning without judgment? That's very different than I'm there for them "no matter what" I have going on, what I'm going through, what I need, what I desire, what I want to do, what matters to me, or what I choose.

To be clear, there's nothing wrong with being there for people. There's nothing wrong with showing up for people the way they need you to that may be a bit different than what you'd normally choose for yourself. But there's a difference between you wanting to be there for others and you believing that you *must* be there for them as someone that you're not in order to maintain the relationship or the beliefs that others have about you. You may be keeping the peace in your relationships when you perform, but how's the peace within you? This is the distinction between presence and performance.

BE PRESENT TO THE DISCOMFORT

Sometimes it's important to let others be uncomfortable with the choices or beliefs that you make if it means you get to live and stand in your truth rather than in their comfort. What would it feel like to stand in your choices without fear of what other people would say or think about you? What would it feel like to be on your side? What would it feel like to take off the protective gear you've been given to wear as a declaration of your compliance to others and society, and instead just be you? This is presence. Being present to who you are. Being present to what matters to you. Being present to what you believe or don't believe. Being present to your emotions, feelings, desires. Being present to you.

Have you ever had a situation like the one I shared above, where you were in a room that you didn't feel you belonged in, so you performed to feel like you fit in? One of the interesting things about performing is that you're often doing it for yourself. The people around you most likely think you're being yourself because if you show up as that person every time, what else would they believe? It's your responsibility to lovingly allow yourself to change what no longer feels true.

HIDING SUCCESS

There are also times where we feel out of place because of our success and we choose to hide, lie, or not share our wins or growth out of fear of not fitting in with the people around us who are doing different things.

As uncomfortable as I felt when I was in that workshop on the Upper East Side, later on when I started to have access to different things in my career and life because of my success, I had a new kind of discomfort. Even though I worked incredibly hard for what I had access to, it took me a long time to believe I deserved it. It took me a long time not to hide what was happening to me or my business. I had confused being humble and staying true to who I was with playing small. I confused being modest with pretending nothing was happening of importance. I was confusing being humble with belittling my triumphs.

Sometimes we perform because we've stepped into a version of ourselves that, although we dreamed and worked for it, we don't have the foundation or language to properly acclimate to our new situation. And perhaps the people around us don't know how to support us either. This can make our achievements feel heavy and therefore we perform because our success feels uncomfortable.

SAFETY

Performance can also feel safe. Sometimes we believe that others don't have the capacity to hold space for our feelings or emotions. Or it can feel scary to think about what people will think about who we really are. I remember when I first started experiencing anxiety, I performed like nothing was happening because I was so afraid and embarrassed to share what I was going through. Sometimes we don't have the words or the language to express how we feel and why we're feeling it, and so we choose to perform instead. It's important to remember to have compassion for yourself as you learn how to communicate in new ways and remind yourself that if performing feels safe, then not performing can feel scary, and it's tough to do what feels scary. The work you're doing to learn that presence is safe is incredibly brave.

PERFORMING EMPTIES
YOUR SUGAR JAR

Performing is a consistent drain to your sugar jar. Your sugar leaks each time you choose to be something other than yourself. This leads to the question: "How do I know who my true self is?" It can feel hard to differentiate between what your truth is and what you were taught to believe your truth is. These are two very different things, but as we grow up, we aren't often given the freedom to explore what we want, but thankfully we can explore it now.

Remember, your kitchen is representative of your life, and all the people, places, and things that you care about have access to your kitchen and your sugar jar, aka you. When you're performing, you may have your lid off in your kitchen because you think it's the *right* thing to do. When your lid is off, you don't have boundaries in place. People are allowed to "pick your brain." They're allowed to borrow items you're not comfortable with. They're allowed to speak to you in hurtful ways because "that's just how they are." And you may be thinking, "Can't I just put the lid on my jar? Won't boundaries solve the problem?" Don't worry, we'll talk about boundaries soon. But remember, if you're in the mode of doing things and showing up for people in a particular way solely based on the fact that you believe it's the right thing to do as a good person or a loving person or a kind person versus because you actually *want* to do it, you'll also put boundaries in place based on those same beliefs that aren't really in alignment with what you need. So before you can even set boundaries that meet your needs, it's helpful to understand what your needs are and what you really believe. And to do that, you will also need to be willing to unlearn performing and embrace presence.

Performance is also one of the instances in which you may be dumping out your own sugar or have cracks in your jar where sugar is pouring out without your awareness of it. When you're living your life as someone you're not, you may not be aware of how draining it is because it feels normal if that's what you always do. But the weight of trying to fit in is bound to cause cracks in your jar. While you're trying to fill yourself up with wellness tools, setting boundaries, and practicing self-care, you may not notice that one of the things you need to do is repair within. You don't need a new jar; there's nothing wrong with the one you've got. You just no longer need to carry the burden of being someone other than you.

Each and every time you choose presence over performance, those cracks in your sugar jar are welded. The weight lessens. You're able to keep more of your sugar for the things you desire.

WE'VE ALL WORN MASKS

It's important to mention that if this resonates with you, you might feel ashamed, I know I did at first. But there is no shame in this. So many of us are pretending without knowing we're pretending and some of us are pretending and know it but don't know how to stop. Some of you are in relationships that you know don't align. Some of you spent years getting a degree to make your family proud even though it isn't what you wanted. Some of you may have had children because you thought that was what you *should* do. Some of you keep friends who don't contribute to your joy. Some of you continue relationships with family members who are toxic and don't feel safe to be around because "that's what family does" or whatever slogan your family uses to make you feel that you need to keep people around who make you feel unsafe or unhappy. The invitation is to go from being a participant in your life to someone who is *living* life the way you really want to live.

SO HOW CAN YOU STOP PERFORMING?

Understand that disappointment is a part of life and relationships. It's uncomfortable but sometimes it's unavoidable. Being honest is healthier than pretending.

Of course, you're not intending to disappoint people, but this is sometimes a by-product of saying yes to yourself over worrying about what matters to others. It's not your job to walk them through their feelings about the way you used to show up in relationship with them. If they're willing to listen, you can communicate how these changes are imperative to you feeling like you.

It's important to gracefully reprogram the idea that people should always be satisfied or happy with the things you say, the things you do, or the way you behave. Even those who care for you will sometimes feel uncomfortable—and that's okay.

Get to know yourself again. When you stop performing, you give yourself permission to get to know yourself on your terms. Instead of thinking "This was how I was raised" before making a decision, you might think "What actually feels good to do next?" Instead of thinking "What would help me fit in" before attending an event, you might think "Just be yourself."

The shift from performing to presence is so powerful because it allows you to feel the freedom that we're taught to believe we'll access through performing. True acceptance of yourself comes through authentically showing up as who you really are, and this can be scary because it's new. Remind yourself that it's a process and that your only job is to show up as you are. There is no correct way to do this other than what feels right to you.

Sometimes we fear that we'll end up alone when we decide to stop performing because we realize we were only fitting in with some of the people around us based on who we're pretending to be. But showing up as you are is a part of the process of getting to know yourself better. Ask yourself: What would it take for me to feel comfortable saying the truth about what matters to me in the groups I spend time in? What do I need so I can feel comfortable being open? If there were no repercussions to walking away from a particular relationship, would I?

Ask yourself: What am I trying to prove when I perform? What am I hoping people will think of me? What about this is already true about me?

Now let's be honest, we've ALL had a "fake it till we make it" moment at one point or another and this can be extremely helpful when we're genuinely aware that we're doing it and the reason that we're doing it. This isn't the same as unconsciously or consciously behaving as something that we're not.

What do you hope people will believe about you based on how you were showing up with them? What have you been taught to believe about people who show up as you do? What would feel more comfortable to you? When have you noticed that you've felt most like yourself?

Ask yourself: How is my peace? You may be keeping the peace around you when you perform, but how is the peace within you?

When do you feel the most at peace? What would it feel like to be able to bring that peace with you **as you**? What limits your peace?

Recognize that it's okay if you don't fit in everywhere. It can be hard to find out that you don't belong in a certain place or with a certain group of people, especially when you really wanted to. But it's harder to be someone that you're not so that you do "fit." Being unapologetically honest with yourself about what you do, why you're doing it, and how you're feeling about all of it is necessary for you to get out of the desire to please others and instead please yourself. And a part of that healing is accepting that you won't fit into every space and that's more than okay.

Ask yourself: Why would I want to be anywhere that I'm not meant to be?

WHAT WOULD PRESENCE OVER PERFORMANCE IN REAL LIFE LOOK LIKE?

- Using the *A* from the S.U.G.A.R. acronym and always checking within.

- Not laughing at jokes that aren't funny to you.

- Telling the uncomfortable truth about how you're feeling when asked.

- Being honest with yourself about the red flags that you're ignoring in the name of "kindness."

- Sharing your excitement about your successes instead of playing them down out of fear.

- Setting boundaries with your own comfort in mind.

- Laughing loudly when you're enjoying a joke.

- Not keeping up with the Joneses—or anyone for that matter— only keeping up with what matters to you.

- Choosing to show up as yourself in all circumstances.

Presence over performance encourages joy. It encourages standing up for yourself. It encourages you to be more like you.

WHAT WOULD THE STORY I SHARED EARLIER LOOK LIKE IF I'D CHOSEN PRESENCE OVER PERFORMANCE?

Would I walk into that Upper East Side event knowing exactly who I was? Mmm . . . maybe a *little*. But the truth is that the story would most likely be similar. The difference would be in the way I talked to myself while I was experiencing those incredibly valid feelings. Instead of saying to myself, "Yasmine, you don't belong here," I'd say, "You're exactly where you need to be in this moment." Instead of saying to myself, "If they find out how much you make, they'll never respect you," I'd say, "Remember, everyone starts somewhere, so be brave and ask the tough questions."

When practicing presence over performance, you won't necessarily be able to step into every experience perfectly composed as your fullest self. There is no perfectionism in this. You may *still* feel worried about what people will think. You may *still* feel like you wish you had that degree or dress or other item where the lingering story still lives in your mind that it would make you appear "better."

Presence over performance doesn't make you perfect; it allows you to be you with grace. When those stories appear when we're doing something new that feels scary, or hanging out with friends, or dating, or any of the many vulnerable things that we do where we have the choice of whether we're going to be ourselves or someone else, we're armed with reminders of why who we **already are** is more than enough. We can also show compassion to ourselves if we unintentionally or unconsciously perform. Remind yourself that you're learning and growing and you can try again next time.

Say It with Me

I'm releasing any part of me that favors performing or pretending for the comfort of others.

I'm committed to loving every part of me exactly as I am.

I knew I was healing when I was willing to release what they desired me to be and choose what I know I'm destined to be.

4

HOW DO YOU FEEL?

It was becoming clearer that I was going to get divorced. If I had to summarize my emotions at the time, my overwhelming feeling was that I'd failed. I was worried about how this decision would affect my daughter's life and I was nervous about the journey ahead. A small part of me thought that because I'd made a decision that I knew was best for me, grief wouldn't be a part of the experience. I was absolutely wrong, as grief was a constant companion for some time. And because I was in my twenties, my community and I hadn't experienced grief in this way yet. This was a learning experience for all of us.

I don't know if people say the "canned" comments that they share with people getting divorced or people breaking up with the thought that it will help them heal faster, but the undertone of all conversations was "There's someone else out there, you'll be fine." It was such a contradiction to be holding the projected emotion of "You'll be fine" with my personal feelings of "You've failed and what am I going to do now?"

I also got a lot of the "There's someone else out there for you" messages and I know it was to help me feel like I wouldn't be alone forever if I didn't want to be, but it always felt like these comments were more for the people who were talking to me rather than for me. I didn't feel that there was room to talk about how I was *really* feeling. And to be honest, I didn't know how I was feeling, nor did I know where to begin to figure that out. I remember googling people who were divorced with a child so I could learn how they coped and to find ways to bring myself peace from the heavy societal weight of shame that I felt.

Anytime you go through an experience that invites you to be seen vulnerably, like divorce, it can be incredibly uncomfortable for those who aren't used to sharing space with you in that way. Before my divorce, I wouldn't have shared how I was *really* feeling, nor would I have desired space for those kinds of conversations. I didn't know how to be vulnerable with myself, nor did I know how to be vulnerable with others. I was in this in-between place of learning that I needed support but also learning how to ask because I didn't know how.

I also remember those moments when I would finally have the guts to try to be honest about how tough it was for me at the time, and I'd get responses back like "Girl, you've got to be willing to move on! Harping over what happened in the past isn't going to help you." I didn't know at the time how to respond to that and say, "I hear you, but do you have the space to hear how I'm scared that I won't be able to move on? I'm still trying to figure this out." It would crush me, and I'd use those experiences where I felt silenced to justify that it wasn't worth it to explore feelings. I thought to myself, *It's much safer to just keep it all in.*

When I look back on this time, I think about three powerful lessons that I learned about community and feelings that I still lean on to this day:

- Ensure that you're speaking to people who've showed you they can hold space for what you need in that moment.

- Sometimes people who love you can't handle where you're at emotionally. In those times, turn to others who can.

- Allow yourself to feel how you feel, no matter what anyone else thinks you should be feeling.

I was doing what I thought was the "right" thing, which was reaching out to people when I needed support. And it's such a lesson to realize that when you ask for support, it won't always show up the way you imagined it, especially if you're not clear on whom you're talking to or what you need. It's hard to share what you need when you don't know how you feel. And it's hard to share how you feel when you don't feel safe doing it.

These lessons were completely unknown to me at the time. Unfortunately, I was internalizing everyone's responses to my experience as additional work for me to do rather than seeing it as their opinion or projection or trigger that I didn't have to carry with me. If someone thought I should've already moved on, for example, then I would think that maybe I was taking too long. If a friend didn't want to discuss something that felt scary or new to me because they didn't think it was that big of a deal, instead of finding another friend to talk to, I shut myself down. I didn't realize that hey, perhaps I need to go within and explore these topics for myself. I just thought, *Shut. it. down.*

I started to believe that it's safer when you don't share your feelings. No one ever explicitly said this to me, nor do I have a memory of a moment where someone looked me in the eyes and said the words "your feelings don't matter." But through multiple encounters like the one I shared above, the message got through to me loud and clear. It felt easier to ignore what I was feeling, and relationships felt lighter when I wasn't bringing anything "heavy" to the table. As a result, I internalized that my feelings didn't matter to me either. I stuffed my emotions down, consciously and unconsciously, because it felt safer to keep them hidden than to do the scary but brave work of sharing them, only to have them be ignored or what felt like ignored.

Through experienced trauma and trauma that was passed down

to me, I learned that it was safer to pay attention to the feelings and emotions going on in the other people around me rather than the ones inside me. Codependency taught me early on that if I could guess or know through hypervigilance what someone else was feeling or needing before they needed it, not only would I be seen as a good person, but I could also try to avoid any potential conflict. Not only did this require me to pretend my feelings of discomfort didn't exist, but it also required putting others' emotions before my own. I believed that monitoring everyone else around me was how you created safety and security. I could never have imagined that my emotions were the road map to building and creating safety and security within me and around me.

Even though divorce is a time where support and encouragement are so necessary, I chose to deal with a lot of the tough times alone. I did receive some support from my community, but mostly I kept them at a distance. I didn't want to receive harsh advice and I also didn't want to "tell my business," which is good practice in terms of not oversharing with the wrong crowd, but it was hard for me to differentiate which "business" was safe to tell and which wasn't. Out of fear of asking the wrong questions, or getting the wrong feedback, I kept quiet.

Our emotions and feelings are more than just our reactions, they're our internal guidance. I had no understanding of how I could cultivate a real connection to myself or others. I was just going through the motions, as so many of us do.

When I work with clients, the thing that's often shared with me is that they wish they knew then, during their past tough times, what they know now so that they could've had an awareness of how truly powerful and capable they really were before making choices that would impact them in ways they couldn't understand yet. We often feel that if we did know, we could've avoided the hard feelings. So many of us feel like we've lost out on the opportunity to live a life that's filled with commitments, friends, and experiences that we're excited for. We believe that because we didn't do all the things we could have then, that there's no room for change or growth now. We rationalize that we can't make certain changes because it would be so different from the current way that our communities or cultures operate. Even if the way things operate is contributing to our dissatisfaction, we still might feel compelled to go with their flow. We may be asking ourselves, "Who am I to think that I can do something different? Who am I to think that things will work out for me?"

It's hard to believe that you have the power to change your life when you don't believe you have permission to admit how uncomfortable you feel right now. Especially if you're currently unhappy while living the life you *thought* you wanted. However, it could also be true that your life could be a by-product of what you felt/feel you were expected to create. Maybe you feel like changing your mind is impossible. Maybe you feel like your partner won't be on board with you, and that's scary. Maybe you feel like you'll have to do it alone and you're tired of "doing it alone." Maybe you don't even know you're uncomfortable, because unbearable has become normal and normal feels better than putting yourself out there and potentially getting it wrong again.

Another thing that can be tough is learning how to differentiate your voice from all the other voices that have been placed inside of you from your parents' voices, friends' voices, and old bosses' voices, just to name a few. The more we pay attention to our internal voice, the clearer and louder it gets. It gets easier knowing when it's our voice speaking or if it's someone else's fear, shame, or judgment talking from within us. Sometimes our feelings get muffled with our stories and other people's beliefs inside of us. This is also why it's so important to be careful whom you allow to speak into your life—about your dreams, goals, desires, and anything you're attempting to manifest into reality. It can be harmful when people speak their fears to us. It can be harmful when people speak their disbelief to us. Even if we walk away thinking that there's no truth to what they said, their lingering voice and negative energy may stay within us. Tending to your sugar jar helps with ensuring that only your sugar remains and that any negative bits that get into your jar from others can be quickly removed.

Learning how you feel is how you get to know yourself on an emotional level. What makes you feel excited? What makes you feel free? What makes you feel loved? This is all about learning more about you, which is the key anyway—you are the key to you. No one else. We won't always get it right, but the more we pay attention, the more we learn. Learning to be gentle with ourselves as we grow and giving ourselves space to figure it out is a part of healing. You're doing it right even when it doesn't go the way you hoped or planned.

I intentionally put this chapter before the boundaries chapter because it can be hard to set healthy boundaries when you don't know how you're feeling. You might think you're making changes because you're making decisions, but actually you're in the same cycle, maintaining the very unhealthy connections that you're trying to adjust. Connection to our feelings gives us clarity, answers that are aligned with what we desire, and flexibility to change our minds, and it can feel more easeful because we know we're doing what we need in the moment. It doesn't mean that it'll be easy, but it can be less complicated when we understand our emotions and intentions, and then set the boundary from that place. To be able to set your boundary, it's important to learn what you want, need, desire, and require, and that comes from having conversations with yourself that invite you to learn about how you actually feel instead of simply reacting based on external relationships and experiences from others. Wisdom from elders and others is priceless, but it's just as important to call on your own wisdom as well.

WHAT DID I UNDERSTAND ABOUT MY EMOTIONS WHEN I LEARNED TO PAY ATTENTION?

- I learned that my anxiety was loud when my voice was quiet.

- I learned that as strong as I was, there was also a gentle and tender part of me that needed care and permission to come forward.

- I learned that I'm not often "behind" on things, I'm often over-committed.

- I learned that I believed I was failing based on a desire to meet goals that were created by me, which also meant that I had the power to change the timeline. These rules or structures were picked up with the desire to be seen, loved, and appreciated.

- I learned that I was overworking for a love I didn't know how to give myself.

- I learned that I had access to vulnerability, and I became stronger the more I leaned into it.

- I learned that the changes I was seeking would require replacing old beliefs with new ones—and that it would take patience and care.

- I learned that I can be heard and understood when I'm talking to the right people.

- I learned that speaking up is a practice, and even though I'm an adult, it's okay if it's new to me.

- I learned that my wisdom was curated not only through my experiences but through my emotions. Without my emotions, my experiences were just things that occurred, not things I endured.

- I learned that my fear of not seeming "humble" was a fear of pride, power, and worth, something I also inherited as a false sense of protection. Playing small doesn't keep me safe.

- I learned that I was going to be let down, and experiencing disappointment was also a practice embroidered in strength, bravery, wisdom, and vulnerability.

EXPLORING YOUR EMOTIONS

You can phrase them as I did above starting with:

- I learned that my _____ (add an emotion or feeling, followed by what you learned).

Or you can start with these questions below (or do both):

- What have you learned as you begin to pay attention to your emotions?

- Is there anything that you're afraid to learn?

- Is there anything that you were taught about feelings that served you in the past, but isn't serving you any longer?

- Are there any emotions that you stuffed down that you're afraid will come up?

- What are you looking forward to as you learn more about how you feel in the present?

SAYS WHO?

I knew I was healing when I began to question where all my beliefs and ideals were coming from. I began to understand that even
though the information may have been coming from people who
loved and cared about me, the details could be tainted with fears,
lack of confidence, lack of faith, and low vibrational energy. To
begin living a life that I had never seen, I had to begin to do some
radical questioning of myself and others, though not necessarily in
conversation with them but internally in conversation with myself.

Who says I **can't** get my dream job in less time? Who says I
can't find a partner who is aligned with beliefs that don't put me in
a box? Who says that I **can't** start again? Who says I **can't** figure out
another way? Who says? WHO SAYS? Ask yourself this question
as often as you need to.

WHEN IN DOUBT, FACT-CHECK

Fact-checking allows you to look at your internal dialogue and
determine whether it's based on evidence or if it's language that's
been passed down to you to remind you of what you can or can't
do and **isn't *actually* true**. Fact-checking is a powerful tool to use
in almost all scenarios where you're unsure whether what you're
telling yourself is the truth or information based on fears or stories
that we've been taught through experience or through society to
believe are true. Or perhaps through stories we've created for

ourselves. It can even help us check what we believe to be the truth, because sometimes our truth is based on untruths. For example, if I believe that I'm a failure because I'm getting divorced, I can confuse me being hard on myself with the truth, especially when there is societal evidence that supports what I'm telling myself. But am I a failure because I'm getting divorced? No, of course not. But I'd have to be willing to challenge my "truth" to realize that what I think is true about myself (being a failure) is not a truth. Fact-checking helps us have these very powerful conversations with ourselves.

Here's an example of fact-checking.

THE STORY

I'm getting divorced and I truly never expected to be in this place. Although I know I'm making the right decision for me, I'm still moving through a lot of emotions. Some people have shared with me that I should just "move on" and that the right person will come along when the time is right. They even want me to stop talking about the hard situations that come up; they've said that I'm "carrying baggage into the next relationship." There seems to be more focus on whom I'll find post-divorce than how I'll feel post-divorce. I feel pressure to do what they're saying partly because I want to get back to the fun parts of life but also because I'm tired of being in these uncomfortable feelings as well. I know they just want me to be happy, but I'd really love it if I could just be where I'm at in this moment.

NOW LET'S BREAK THE STORY DOWN
Your Friends'/Family's Truth

- You're getting divorced.

- When getting divorced, moving on as quickly as possible is what helps.

- You should be concerned about the "baggage" you're potentially taking into your next relationship.

- Stop talking about painful experiences; it doesn't help you move on.

[NOTE: It may not be that the people who are telling you to move on are telling you this because they don't care about how you feel. They might believe that if you appear to have moved on, by no longer talking about the tough experiences, then poof—the problem is fixed! But grief and loss don't often work that way.]

Your Current Truth

- I'm getting divorced and it's painful.

- This experience isn't something I felt prepared for.

- I should try to move on like I'm being encouraged to do so that I stop burdening those around me, but I really need support right now.

The Fact-Checked Truth

- I'm getting divorced and it's painful.

- Moving on is helpful when I reenter the dating world, but I'm not there yet.

- Divorce has left me with a lot to unpack, and there's nothing wrong with wanting to take my time working through it.

- Most of us haven't prepared for painful experiences, and it's okay to be unsure while moving through them.

- Moving on faster than I'm ready to or hiding how I feel isn't helpful. I can share that I need more time and find safe spaces/friends/a therapist to unpack my feelings with.

- Just because someone cares about me, it doesn't mean they're equipped to handle everything that I'm going through. It's okay if my feelings about my divorce feel big to those around me, too.

Going forward, I can ask my support system if they have space for the tough thing(s) that I'd like to talk about and share what I need from them clearly. For example, "Do you have space to hear me talk about my fears around co-parenting? I'd really love it if you could listen, as I don't need advice at the moment. Let me know if you have space for this."

The Fact-Checked Story

I'm going through a painful experience that I never imagined I'd be going through. Even though it's difficult for me, and for those around me to see me this hurt, I'm doing the right thing by processing my feelings and experiences at a pace that feels good for me. My friends and family remind me that "there are other people out there" or that "you'll be okay" and I know they're trying to cheer me up. It's important that I share how their comments make me feel while also sharing what I need from them in these moments. It's also important that I'm honest with myself if they're unable to be there for me in the ways that I need them to be so that I can find the alternative support. There are disappointments in life, and although it's uncomfortable, I can get through it.

Conclusion

Yes, society has a lot to say about people who get divorced. And a lot of people have beliefs about how one should move through the process of divorce. But it doesn't mean that we must own society's beliefs, our friends' or family's beliefs, or anyone else's for that matter. Sometimes only we understand that we're doing what's best for us. It's important to continue checking in with ourselves, asking ourselves how we feel, and remaining attached to our emotions. It's there that we'll always find our truth.

P.S. This fact-checking exercise is for you to process any feelings or stories, and you don't have to share with anyone that you don't want to.

GETTING TO KNOW YOUR INTUITION

Intuition is sometimes also called your gut, your knowing, your spirit, God, the universe, or any other list of names that we use to describe the part of us that appears to know what we need and how to keep us away from harm, no matter what. We get to decide whether we want to listen or not, but the more we listen and the more we are in conversation with our intuition, the clearer and louder it gets.

Think about the times you've used the sayings "Something told me to . . ." or "I could feel it in my gut . . ." Those were all moments that your intuition was speaking to you and you responded, whether you chose to listen or not; it was still communication. Our intuition is often the part of us giving feedback about people, places, and commitments that come our way without the heart or the head being involved, meaning we're getting the information straight—no chaser. Intuition rarely deals in the could be, should be, or might be, and it also rarely offers any advice that puts us in a position to betray ourselves. This is one of the main reasons we don't often listen to our intuition, because it will tell us no even if it means walking away from our "dream" person, "dream" opportunity, or any other "dream" that isn't aligned.

If you struggle with connecting to your intuition or your energy in general, let's do "the crowded party" exercise. I'd like you to think about a time when you were in a room full of people. There is music blaring from the speakers, people are walking around talking and perhaps even bumping into others with pleasantries being exchanged. It's loud and there is a lot being expressed. But suddenly, without knowing which direction it's coming from, you get the **feeling** that someone is staring at you. You don't know how you know that in this room of crowded people; you just know that you can **feel** someone's energy being directed at you. Probably without even thinking, you start to look around to sense where this is coming from, and most of us have had that moment where we immediately lock eyes with the person who was looking at us and then we both look away trying to pretend it didn't happen.

This is not only evidence of how clear our intuition can be, but it's also evidence of how clearly we can feel someone else's energy coming in our direction. It's also evidence that our intuition is working without us even being "tuned in," and thank goodness, right? Our intuition is on and plugged in even if we are unable to fully tap into it the way we want to in the beginning.

A question that I'm always asked is "How do I know the difference between my intuition and fear?" Here's an example of how to tell the difference:

- Fear might sound like: "I shouldn't be doing this, even though I want to, because what if something happens? What if someone finds out? What if . . ."

- Intuition might sound more like: "I can feel that I don't want to do this. It doesn't mean that this commitment is wrong, it's just not for me. It's a clear no."

- Intuition always feels more concrete and certain than fear, even when our fear feels real.

GETTING TO KNOW
YOUR DISCERNMENT

Discernment is different from intuition, but the two go hand in hand. Discernment is your spiritual intellect, and it allows you to make decisions based on the information you're receiving from your intuition but also through your knowledge, wisdom, ancestral guidance, and/or your experiences. Discernment, like intuition, takes practice and time to build self-trust because your decisions will be based on what YOU are feeling.

How many times have you known what you should do but instead poll/ask others around you what they would do, hoping to find enough tallies of people who agree with you rather than believing that what you're already feeling is right? That your answer is already enough? To be clear, it's okay to ask for help and to have discussions with others about what they think. I leaned heavily on my community to be there for me as a single mom who needed support, advice, and encouragement. It's completely okay to ask for information from others because sometimes our intuition may be giving us the nudge to ask just the right person, and when we check in with ourselves (aka use our discernment) and decide we should ask them, we get just the right information, referral, or answer that we're looking for. Handed right to us from an external source. Have you ever had a moment like that? Where someone, whom perhaps you don't even know, ends up giving you the information that you needed and you felt "Wow, I was meant to meet them in this moment!"

Those divine or universe alignments happen in ways that sometimes we can't even predict or explain. Sometimes intuition and discernment will say, "Hey, you'll find exactly what you need from them, so ask." That's different than your intuition and discernment saying "Do this," and you responding with "Let me check with others and make sure that my knowing is correct." No one can tell you for sure if your intuition or discernment is right or wrong; that's a personal journey for you to learn. Others can only share their thoughts based on the information you've given them, and what they're telling you, even if it's phrased as "what you should do," it's really what *they* would do. And what they would do may not be for you.

Wanting answers from others is a normal part of being human. But it's also an indication that it's hard to trust yourself. Self-trust is built through understanding that when you make mistakes, there will be another side and you'll get through it even if it doesn't work out the way you hoped. The misconception is that self-trust is built through perfection and never making mistakes. The truth is, you'll learn more about what feels good for you by making decisions for yourself and adjusting as needed. It's powerful to be willing to get it wrong and then try again.

In truth, it can be scary to make decisions based on your intuition and discernment because so many of us have learned to trust external reactions rather than internal ones. Be honest with yourself about knowing that you don't know what you don't know. It's hard to grow when you're unable to be honest with yourself. And make space for gentle practice and learning more by allowing yourself to be a student.

When learning the difference between your fear and your discernment, here's an example:

- Fear might sound like: "I should just do what they asked of me so that there aren't any issues or problems."

- Discernment might sound like: "Something doesn't feel right about what I've been asked to do. This doesn't feel aligned for me."

It's tough when you struggle with self-trust because decisions you made in the past didn't work out, so you might be afraid that it will happen again. Discernment helps us learn how to make decisions based on our truth, with the knowledge that we can be there for ourselves if our plans fall through.

"INVENTORY" FOR YOUR SUGAR JAR

Your feelings are essentially the inventory system for your jar. Feeling good? You may not need more sugar at this time, and your jar is right where it should be for the moment. Not feeling so good? Your jar may be running low on sugar and you may be overcommitted or in an uncomfortable situation.

If you never realized that you have full control of your life and that your feelings show you where your discomfort is, you may not know that your jar belongs to you. Your family may have had a community kitchen where everyone was encouraged to put their jars together so that anyone who needed anything was allowed to jump in and take it. Or you may have decided on a community kitchen with your partner or friends, because you didn't know that your jar was yours alone. And to be clear, if there is a community-kitchen situation, your individual kitchen still exists, it's just being neglected without care and attention.

Now that you know that your jar and kitchen belong to you, you get to decide what you want and what that will look like for you. You get to release the desires that others have for you to fulfill for them and instead choose what you want to fulfill for yourself. You get to admit when you're upset, when you're tired, when you need more, when you need less, or any other vast array of options. When your sugar jar is placed on a sturdy foundation in your kitchen, where it belongs, you give yourself the power to change your mind. Our power lies in knowing that we can do this. This sets the stage for building healthy boundaries, healthy relationships, and healthy lives.

When you think about your emotions, where, if anywhere, do you feel sensations in your body? When do your shoulders tighten? When does your throat or mouth get dry? When do you start to fidget with your hands or feet? When does your body feel more relaxed or anxious?

Paying attention to how you physically feel when you tune in to your emotions may also help you to learn more about how your body is reacting to your feelings.

Paying attention to whether your energy is stagnant or flowing is an indication of how you feel. Paying attention to whether you feel light or heavy is an indication of how you feel. Imagine holding a sugar cube, where there is no flow. It's still sugar, but most likely it will feel heavier than that same amount of loose sugar in your hand. The form our sugar takes matters.

In another example, let's imagine our kitchen again, and suddenly smoke starts to appear, causing a fire alarm to go off. Obviously, this is a cause for concern, but a friend or family member or teacher or mentor, no matter how well-intentioned, sees the smoke as well and says, "It's fine." There may be several other people in your kitchen who are continuing to live their lives in the smoke, noticing the discomfort it causes, noticing how it's harder to see clearly because it takes intention to ignore something that's right in front of us. But they've learned how to operate without attachment to all their senses. And now they're asking you to do it, too. They ask you to ignore the smoke, to ignore the alarm, to not try to find out the cause, but instead to keep moving and adjust and learn how to live with the smoke present. This is conforming to the discomfort. When an alarm is going off and smoke appears, we should figure out how we can stop the smoke that's causing the alarm. Finding the cause allows us to create the change that makes the environment comfortable.

Your sugar should be allowed to flow. Flow is ease. Flow is freedom. Flow is not conforming. Flow is not staying with the pack.

The old definition of "go with the flow" invites us to ignore our feelings, but when we do this, it doesn't make the discomfort go away; we've just stopped paying attention.

HOW CAN I FILL MY JAR?

I CHOOSE YOU

Choosing what you want for yourself and your life based on your beliefs and feelings is one of the greatest acts of self-love there is. Choosing yourself will require you to prioritize your needs over what others need from you. Choosing yourself will bring more joy into your decisions as opposed to resentment.

Deciding to choose yourself may piss people off. Our society is not yet wired with the idea that people should be allowed to make the decisions they want to. People who choose themselves are often called selfish, among other names, and many people are afraid of choosing themselves for fear that the people around them will believe they are self-centered.

But choosing yourself doesn't mean that you won't choose others as well. And it doesn't mean that you are participating in selfish behavior. It means asking yourself, "Does it feel aligned? Am I excited to be a part of it?" And if the answer is no, choosing yourself means figuring out how to make it work in a way that feels better for you so that you're living a life you enjoy rather than a life that you tolerate.

When I shared about my divorce earlier, I shared that I thought I was a failure because my marriage was ending, but the truth was that I thought I was failing based on society's definitions of what "success" and "winning" were. From my place of truth, the decision to end a relationship that wasn't working was proof of my willingness to choose myself. Sometimes choosing yourself looks like letting go of something that you never imagined you would ever have to. We aren't taught to do this. We're taught to suck it up, to suffer (silently), and to not complain. We're taught to do what our parents would've done. We're taught to make it fit when it doesn't fit and to make it work when it's clear that it no longer does. And if we're unable to do those things, then we're taught that we're outcasts from society, proof of not being worthy of love again. And that's just not the case.

Did my jar instantly fill up after making the decision to divorce? No, it took time to get to know myself. I had to learn to make different decisions. I had to unlearn unhealthy cycles. I had to say no to environments that were toxic for me. Over time I learned how to stand in alignment with what was best for me.

SETTING INTENTIONS

Now, let's set some intentions based on what you've learned in this chapter.

Your intentions will be different than when you set goals, as these won't have a time frame. They won't be SMART goals, and they won't be measured based on anything other than your feelings.

You'll ask yourself: Is this intention I set for myself still aligned? Or does it need to change to fit what I need now?

Is this intention I set for myself still aligned? Or does it need to change now that I have more information? Remember, you're allowed to change your mind.

Sample Intentions

- I choose to grow despite what society says will limit me.

- I choose to build a community where I feel comfortable being myself.

- I choose a life that is built on beliefs that serve my desires and needs.

Say It with Me

I'm committed to using my feelings and emotions as a road map to what is aligned and what I need to shift.

I have the power and agency to change my mind at any time.

Other people, no matter how well-intentioned, don't get to say what's possible for me.

5

BOUNDARIES
AND BARRIERS

While teaching a workshop a few years ago, I asked the guests to write down where they believed their sugar went each day. As they wrote, I talked them through the potential ways their sugar might be used, like while running errands, taking care of the kids, working, or any potential commitment they might have. After a few minutes of this, I asked everyone to look over their jar and check to see if they felt they were ready to move on to the next part of the exercise. Everyone gave me a collective head nod. I then shared: "Before we move forward, I'd like everyone to look down at their jars and see if you named yourself as one of the places that your sugar goes." A collective groan moved across the vast room of more than one hundred people, which shook me to my core. Not a single person had placed themselves on the list of where their sugar goes. Not one. When we put healthy boundaries in place, we ensure that we're much higher up on the list.

Boundaries are essential to our healing and they ensure that the healing work we do lasts. There's really no other way to be certain that you can live the way you truly want to without setting boundaries. This can feel hard because for many of us when we think about boundaries, we might think it's an opportunity to get the people, places, and things around us to do what we want them to do. But boundaries aren't about controlling other people. Boundaries invite you to be intentional about yourself and what you sign up for or allow. *Boundaries are not ultimatums; they're opportunities for all involved to be clear about what's needed.*

My definition of boundaries is that they are the rules or structures that we put in place that manage the way we interact with the people, places, things, and commitments that we have in our lives. Boundaries are important as they help us to control the way we live our lives, how we interact with others, and how they are allowed to interact with us. By setting boundaries we ensure the protection of our health and mental wellness by communicating how our time, attention, money, and all the aspects of us can and will be utilized. Boundaries are how we communicate, through conversations or actions, what we're comfortable with.

The most frequent interaction we'll have with our sugar jar is taking our lid off and putting it on. Our decision about who gets some of us, whether it is a tangible or energetic part of us, impacts the way we feel daily. For many of us, it can be scary or anxiety-inducing to think about whether to say yes or no because even though we may know what we want, we still might feel nervous about how other people will react. Taking your lid off is a boundary and it means that the person or commitment has access to you. Keeping your lid on is also a boundary and it means that the person or commitment doesn't have access to you in that moment. And because we're in charge of defining our boundaries, it matters that we're comfortable with them and that they help us feel safe.

Boundaries aren't necessarily absolute, which means we can still live in the gray areas. Our "I don't know" is still allowed, which means we can decide not to take action until we know more. Even though "I don't know" or "I'm not sure" isn't a clear yes or no, it's still a boundary when we give explicit and clear direction. Your boundaries can leave room for you to learn more, to understand more, to not move forward, to look backward, or anything else that you decide is necessary. You can always say "I don't know, and I'll get back to you when I do" or "I'm not sure, so I'm going to opt out until I know more."

When we're uncomfortable with something, and we don't clearly communicate our boundaries, people don't know what we actually need, and they can begin to make up stories about what they think we need. Boundaries help us clearly share what we're uncomfortable with and what we'll need to feel comfortable. Boundaries ensure that we prioritize ourselves so that even when we're supporting others, we're not compromising ourselves.

People often wonder, "How are my uncommunicated actions boundaries?" There's a misconception that we *have* to tell people who might be impacted by our boundary every single time we set new ones, and that's not always the case. When people are starting their journey with boundaries, I always tell them that having uncommunicated boundaries is a great place to begin because you're able to enforce what you need without having to have a conversation.

For example, a few years ago, I decided that I would turn the "do not disturb" on my phone to after 8:00 p.m. so that I wouldn't get any calls, texts, or notifications unless it was an emergency. This is an uncommunicated boundary because I've closed the lid on my sugar jar after 8:00 p.m., specifically for any phone inter-actions, without having to share it with anyone. I don't have to text all my friends to let them know that I'm doing this, nor do I need to explain why. This is a boundary that I'm setting for me. Now if a friend asks why I didn't respond to a message, I can share that it's because I don't use my phone after a certain time. I don't have to apologize for my boundary. I don't have to feel bad about it either. And guess what? Over time, my friends stopped texting me after 8:00 p.m. and we'd chat during the day or during other times when we were both available. It's also important to empha-size that my not being available after 8:00 p.m. doesn't mean that my friends have to text or call *only* when I'm available. I now must find a time that they're available that also works for me. Boundaries are often about compromise, and even with uncommunicated boundaries, you can do this.

It's also important to share that boundaries start with **you** first and the pressure you may feel to have all the right words to say to others gets in the way of getting started. When you're starting to set boundaries, it can be tough to know where to begin setting them in relationships. Without ever having a conversation with someone else, you can begin to make decisions for yourself and implement boundaries that positively impact your life. Setting healthy boundaries is self-love. It's the preserver of our peace. It's the protector of our joy. Often, the freedom we're seeking in our lives will come from the boundaries we choose.

Sometimes setting boundaries means grieving relationships that will never be what we prayed they could. Sometimes boundaries look like letting go of things or people who won't change. Sometimes boundaries look like making positive changes in our routines by eliminating things that aren't working. Sometimes boundaries look like telling people what they can and can't do to us.

Boundaries can be applied in every area of our lives, and as you can see, the presence or absence of them impacts how we feel. People without boundaries are less likely to slow down enough to take time for themselves. People without boundaries are more likely to harbor resentment because of times that they've over-given. People without boundaries are more likely to be in relationships with people that don't have reciprocity.

But just because you've lived life so far without or with very few boundaries, it doesn't mean this is what your life must be forever.

A lot of us truly fear what others may think when we start putting boundaries in place for the first time. But it's important to know that if setting boundaries triggers people to leave you, then their love may have been conditional on you never growing. When you're in unhealthy relationships, you're more likely to have your ability to say no reprimanded. When you choose healthy relationships, you're more likely to have your ability to say no be seen as a brave and necessary act, while also having what you need honored. Even in healthy relationships there still may be questions about what your boundaries mean, and that's okay. You can always discuss why you're putting certain boundaries in place without making the boundary itself a debate.

For example, if you try to set a boundary at your job that you don't want to stay late at work more than two days a week, you're probably going to have to explain the reason you've put that boundary in place to your supervisor. Explaining to them that staying late more than two days a week puts stress on you is explaining **why** you decided to set the boundary. Getting into a conversation about whether you'd be able to change the number from two days to three days shifts the discussion from you explaining the boundary to you potentially changing the boundary. In this situation, and in many other cases, you might decide to change the boundary and compromise, after deciding if it will work well for everyone involved. In other situations, you might decide that the boundary isn't movable and therefore not change or shift the boundary in any way. The most important takeaway here is to understand the type of conversation you're having so that you don't walk away wondering what happened to your boundary and why it feels like it was smashed to pieces by the end.

During a virtual wellness training session that I hosted with a corporate organization, we got on the topic of boundaries in the workplace. One employee brought up the subject of meetings and said, "Since we're on the topic of boundaries, I wanted to share that it would be great if we could have some boundaries implemented at work regarding meetings. As an introvert, the meeting culture here doesn't really make space for how I work. It would be great if people weren't shamed for not having the energetic ability to keep up with all the meetings and phone calls plus their work. It would be great if I and all introverts were still seen as professional even if we opted out of certain meetings or calls because of how draining they can be and how they distract us from doing our actual job."

The session went quiet after that, and if you're an introvert like me, you'll know why. We (introverts) have been thinking this **forever,** and if you're also like me, you've even tried to say something about it a few times at your job, but I've never heard it shared so honestly. I'll admit I was a bit nervous for her because it was the longest five seconds ever and no one was cosigning for her yet and everyone's faces were blank. I always like to give a tiny bit of time for someone to jump in before I do, and as soon as I was about to speak, her actual boss stepped in and said, "Wow, I've never thought of what you just said in that way. I always thought people didn't want to be in meetings to find a way to get out of work, but I never thought about how meetings can drain you from being able to do your work, because as an extrovert, meetings revitalize me and my creativity. I need to rethink how meetings look going forward."

After this, there was a flood of commentary from other introverts sharing how they'd also like their team to think about implementing boundaries that supported an environment where people felt like their well-being was considered at work, while also understanding that there would be times when everyone would have to attend meetings even if it was uncomfortable. What mattered to almost everyone in the session was that they were able to be seen and heard and that some of their leadership chimed in and supported them. Even though some of the leadership team was extroverted and didn't fully understand where the introverts were coming from, they were willing to try and often that's what really matters. This is an example of having a tough conversation about a boundary that's needed, which you may not have the authority to set, like in a work environment, and still choosing to have the conversation anyway.

Other times, we have clear evidence that the people we're in relationship with or that we have commitments to aren't willing or able to understand us or meet us where we are, and we may still choose not to set boundaries out of fear of losing them. Recognizing that you aren't saving people or relationships by giving them more than you have is hard. Why do we think if someone does a particular behavior with someone else that they wouldn't do that same behavior with us? Why do we believe them when they tell us "you'll be different" and that we'll receive the respect that the other people in their lives haven't? Or perhaps we didn't have any evidence before the commitment or relationship started, and we were completely blindsided by the lack of reciprocity. Or perhaps we hoped that because we love them or care for them, we would be seen differently.

Ultimately, we believe them because we *have to* in order to be able to stay in our discomfort. If we admitted the reality of the situation, we'd have to admit that we're uncomfortable and make a change. Denial or lack of acceptance keeps us stuck, but it also keeps us with people and commitments that aren't serving us. And even though they aren't serving us, change can be scary, especially when we don't want to lose them.

It's hard to admit this, but we ignore the truth because we want them, or those opportunities, more than we want to choose ourselves. I have certainly been there, where I thought choosing someone I loved was choosing myself. Or I believed that allowing a "friend" to be harmful to me was allowing them to "be themselves." Or I thought overworking was a part of my personality. I didn't realize it was keeping me from myself. I was hoping and praying it would help me find myself, as so many of us do. We say no to setting boundaries. We say no to the tough conversations. And we do that in the name of hope. As in "I hope making this sacrifice to not choose myself pays off." But it rarely does. Hope is important and valuable and necessary. But hope is not the same as truth and it's tough work, but when we learn to hold hope while holding truth, we can be there for ourselves and others in a more loving way.

Hope embodies our desires and sometimes our desires are not based in reality. We can desire someone to change, and it can also be true that they haven't shown any sign that change is happening. This is different than manifestation, or goal setting, or the laws of attraction. We are not able to will other people to be who we want them to be. In the absence of boundaries, we are following them and ignoring ourselves.

Allowing your discomfort with setting boundaries to change who you are does nothing for your growth. You have to ask yourself: Are people not honoring my boundaries? Or am I saying yes when I mean no? Are people not honoring my boundaries or am I not putting them there in the first place? When we're honest with ourselves about our behavior and theirs, we can learn what doesn't belong to us, but more importantly we recognize what our responsibilities are. Once we know what we can change, we can empower ourselves to do it through our boundaries.

Boundaries are loving things, and although they are firm and can be shocking, they're not used to inflict pain. Instead, they usually help to alleviate the continuation of harm. Boundaries can be tough, but they are fully your responsibility. No one will respect your boundaries if you don't. Boundaries keep you from carrying what never belonged to you in the first place.

BARRIERS

You may feel like you've always been able to keep out the toxic or draining people. You may feel like you have a handle on saying no with a capital H-E-L-L. But perhaps there are other boundaries, like your personal boundaries, that are harder to keep up with. Perhaps choosing yourself and doing what you said you were going to do for you feels a bit tougher. Perhaps saying yes when help is offered feels impossible.

When we set a boundary that keeps the unsafe stuff out, like being used or overworking, but it also prevents the good stuff from having access to us, like receiving help and support from safe people and resources, we have created a barrier. It's easy to confuse the two because we might feel safer with both choices than we did before there was anything in place to protect us. But when we choose barriers over boundaries, we prevent flexibility in our choices and instead we set absolutes.

EXAMPLES OF CHOOSING BARRIERS
OVER BOUNDARIES

Barrier: "I'm done dating. I won't ever allow myself to be hurt like that again."

Changing this barrier to a boundary: "That last dating experience was really tough. One of the uncomfortable parts of dating is being vulnerable and sometimes getting hurt. In the future, I'll pay closer attention to any red flags, but I'm so proud of myself for getting back out there when I was ready. I won't continue to date people who hurt me in the future."

Barrier: "That's the last time I'll ever put my creative work out there."

Changing this barrier to a boundary: "It hurts that I put my work out there and didn't receive what I was hoping for. In the future, I'll try to be clearer with myself about my expectations and make the best decision based on what I need. Next time, I'll ask for support from friends so that I can have a circle around me to help me feel safe while doing something brave. I'll continue to share my work in ways that make me feel safe."

Barrier: "Every time I trust a new friend, they always let me down. No one is getting that close to me again."

Changing this barrier to a boundary: "I'm disappointed that I trusted them and they let me down. I was excited to have them in my life. In the future, I'll wait to get to know someone better before I allow them 'friend access' in my life. I won't stay in friendships where there isn't trust and safety and I'll slowly build trust and safety in new friendships."

Of course, you're allowed to decide that you don't ever want to do something ever again. But sometimes we're unclear that we've set a barrier because we're hoping to keep ourselves safe, but we might be pushing away what we truly desire.

Think of boundaries as your clear glass sugar jar. The clear jar prevents others from reaching the sugar inside, but you can still see through the jar. When you have healthy boundaries in place, you can see everything clearly and still access your sugar—aka yourself—if needed. You also recognize that the lid keeps your sugar inside the jar as another boundary. The parameters are very clear, and you understand the purpose. Even if no one else fully understands why your jar remains closed when it does, you do. When we have healthy boundaries in place, we understand why we've made the decisions we have. This doesn't mean we can't change our minds in the future, but if we decide to choose something different, it's a lot easier to make those changes when we understand where we're starting from.

When barriers are in place, instead of a clear glass jar you might have a tinted-glass jar. Yes, it keeps people from seeing what's inside the jar, but if others can't see in the jar, neither can you. A tinted jar also keeps the light out. Yes, it keeps people from knowing what you have, but it also makes it harder for you to see what you have. Yes, it may keep people away because they can't see the goodness that's inside, but you may also forget the goodness that's there, too. Barriers keep you from being able to access yourself because in the process of making it hard for others to have access to you, you make it tougher for you to have access to you. We often put barriers in place after being hurt, as a safety response.

It's important to know that it's okay to choose barriers on the way to boundaries. It's okay to do what you feel will grant you safety.

What's more important is the ability to have the internal conversation with yourself about why you have barriers and how they may be making it harder for you to see you.

ASK YOURSELF:

- Why does it feel safer to not be seen than to let others in with limits?

- When did I learn to set barriers?

- Why do barriers feel like a safer option?

- Do I find that I'm able to say yes to the good things as often as I'm able to say no to the things that don't work?

- Do I find that most of my boundaries are based on fears?

- Do I feel stuck even though I set boundaries? What feels stuck?

It's important to remember that if something makes you uncomfortable, you're allowed to set a boundary to protect yourself. It's also important to know that the boundary could just be needed around that specific person or experience, and that you don't necessarily need the tint on your jar as a blanket barrier for everything or everyone. Feel free to put the tint on when certain folks are around but be willing to let the light in when it's safe.

EXAMPLES OF BARRIERS

- Not allowing people to be there for you.

- Believing you are "stronger" than others and therefore don't need help.

- Being unwilling to receive compliments, asking yourself, "What's the catch?"

- Having a "no new friends" mantra.

- Making blanket statements about a particular group of people based on the experience you had with one or a few people from that group (for example, "My last partner was an Aries, and they hurt me, so now I don't deal with Aries anymore.").

P.S. I'm an Aries Sun, so don't worry, I'm just using my own sign as an example. ☺

Barriers are always an invitation for you to dig deeper and figure out what fears, hurts, or discomfort is keeping you from living your life as fully as it would be if these barriers were not in place. Boundaries replace barriers by providing safety with flexibility. You'll always know if you have a boundary rather than a barrier if there is flexibility. We're aiming for "I didn't like that feeling, so I'm going to be clear about what I need" rather than "I didn't like that feeling, so I'm never going to let anyone get that close to me again."

THINGS WE THINK ARE
BOUNDARIES BUT AREN'T

Subliminal messages are not acts of love and they're also not a safe way to get messages across. They're a form of passive-aggressive unhealthy behavior that is bound to sabotage even the stronger relationships.

Weaponizing boundaries makes other people feel unsafe with us, and they should not be used as a way to attack or harm others. Boundaries allow us to exist in healthy relationships.

Ultimatums aren't boundaries as they attempt to force people to do what we want them to do. Boundaries are opportunities for people to meet us where we are.

Debates aren't boundaries. Boundary violations will happen, and in those circumstances, tough conversation and even arguments may occur. But you're not obligated to debate whether your boundaries are right or wrong for others, and neither are they with you. Debates are not the same as compromise.

"Getting people back," aka revenge, isn't a boundary and usually falls under the barrier category. If someone harms you, you may be tempted to harm them back. And this is normal because you're human. But getting revenge on others isn't a boundary and it's an energetic leak, dumping sugar out of your jar to focus on an unhealthy way of attempting to manage your emotions. We've all been there, and you can forgive yourself or seek forgiveness (if you desire) from those whom you may have harmed. But this still doesn't deal with the boundaries that need to be put in place and instead creates more harm and potential confusion.

Uncommunicated expectations are often mistaken for boundary violations. But others can't violate a boundary that they don't know exists. Ask yourself: Have my boundaries been violated? Or have my uncommunicated expectations not been fulfilled?

Ghosting and specifically using silence as a weapon is not a boundary, it's a barrier. It's tough to have conversations with others, and sometimes we don't want to talk to them. But the silent treatment or disappearing from the lives of people we're committed to doesn't always solve the problem. Of course, sometimes space is needed, but the important thing is to check in with yourself about whether you're taking space or hoping to harm them with your space.

[NOTE: There will be times where immediately removing people from your life, without a conversation, is the safest boundary you can set, and in those situations, do what's best for you. This definition of ghosting or the silent treatment doesn't apply to abusive relationships.]

FROM FOMO TO YOLO

Sometimes, we decide not to put boundaries in place because we fear we might miss out on good times or because of others' comments about our choices. During a group workshop, I was once asked, "If I put boundaries in place, when will I ever have a good time? When will it just be easy? When will I get to just enjoy life without having to worry about the tough stuff?" These are super-valid questions and we all might feel this way at one time or another while navigating boundaries in our closest relationships. I shared with her and the group: "I know it can feel tough when you're putting new boundaries in place and your relationships are all going through adjustments. But when we honor our boundaries, we have a better time in our relationships. When we honor our boundaries, we don't always have to worry about the tough stuff, because we're ready and willing to say what we need when it's necessary. And when we honor our boundaries, our relationships can become more easeful. Some people will choose to continue to love us while understanding our needs, or they may decide to leave. And even though endings can be tough, it's lighter on us than having relationships that aren't working and that drain us just for the sake of having them."

Instead of feeling like you might miss out on a friend, opportunity, or experience if you decide to put boundaries in place, you can invite yourself to think about all that you can and will gain by choosing to uphold what matters to you. Yes, you may need to take the time to grieve the loss of a relationship, and there's nothing wrong with taking the time you need. But it doesn't mean you should stay out of fear. Fear of missing out, aka FOMO, energy in relationships and commitments leads to you saying yes because you feel that if you don't, you're the lone one out and don't fit in. My definition of you only live once, aka YOLO, energy ensures that you make decisions in alignment with you because your time is precious! You always have room for mistakes, "just because" decisions, and those FOMO decisions. But it ensures that YOU and your needs are a prioritized part of the discussion.

THE FEAR

The Question: "What will people think about me when I start to set boundaries?"

People might think you've changed. They're right and changing isn't a negative thing.

People might think you don't care about them anymore. It may be true that you're unable to continue to care for them in the same ways you did before you set boundaries.

People may say that you're unkind now. Many people may believe that kindness is associated with always saying yes, but this isn't a definition that you have to agree to.

People may think that you think you've "made it" and that you're acting "Hollywood" or "brand new." Boundaries won't change what people choose to think about you, but they do change the way you think about yourself, and that's honestly what matters.

It's okay for people to have questions or fears, but that's also not your work to manage. They might ask: "Are we still friends?" "Do you still love me?" "Have I done something wrong?" It can be scary to think about all the potential questions you'll get from others. But the truth is you're allowed to answer their questions while still having autonomy over yourself.

BOUNDARIES CAN FEEL LIKE A THREAT

Other people won't always like the boundaries that we set. Sometimes people will choose to internalize our boundaries as a personal attack on them. Some people will ignore our boundaries altogether. Of course, it's not our work to process their emotions for them, but we're still responsible for ensuring that our guidelines are clear to them and to us. For situations where people feel hurt by our boundaries, we can remember how confusing or nerve-racking it may have felt (or still feels) when others set boundaries with us, and this can help us be more empathetic and understanding to the way people react to us. At the same time, it's important to understand our limits around other people's reactions to our boundaries and to not overextend ourselves beyond what feels reasonable to us.

Other people will have their boundaries, too, and it's important, especially in relationships and partnerships, to understand what everyone needs so you can compromise or honor those needs. Of course sometimes we decide that their boundary is too much and we choose to walk away.

There will be times where you're clear that you're not interested in compromising, and that's also okay. Understanding that your boundary may be hard for others doesn't mean that you should eliminate it. When we bend to meet others, when we already know that what they're asking won't work for us, we decide that their comfort is more important than ours. Ask yourself: Is it worth it not to follow my intuition and boundaries and face the consequence of ignoring my truth?

LOCKING YOUR KITCHEN DOOR
AND CLOSING YOUR SUGAR JAR

When you think about your kitchen again, your boundaries are all the supportive materials that allow everything in it to stand while also doubling as the access points. Boundaries are the door to the kitchen, boundaries are the foundation of the house, boundaries are the countertop that your sugar jar lives on, boundaries are the lid of your jar, and boundaries are the jar itself. Why? Because boundaries have many layers and there are many ways that we can put them in place to protect ourselves. If you don't want someone to have access to your jar, you might want to ask yourself why they have access to the kitchen at all. Does the countertop your jar lives on feel sturdy or wobbly? Asked another way, are your boundaries firm or are they unclear and lack stability? Just like you would repair anything in a kitchen in real life, you have the same freedom in your energetic kitchen. You have complete authority, even in the moments where you've been taught to believe that you don't.

Sugar can be used for many things. It can be used to sweeten tea, it can be used to bake cookies, it can be used to make caramel, it can be used to make candy, and it can even be used as a skin exfoliant. It's super versatile. Your sugar can also be used for many things. Sugar is energy and so it is our money, our time, our attention, our wisdom, our expertise, our gifts, and our abilities. We use our sugar to be present in all these things and we also use our sugar to help us increase our wisdom, money, and everything that we desire in our lives. But it takes sugar to increase our sugar. This means that it takes time and energy to fill our jars. When our intentions are clear, we're able to set boundaries that free our sugar to do all the things we've said yes to. When our intentions are unclear, our boundaries are most likely unclear as well and therefore our sugar usage is also unclear.

Before we even get to the question of whether we want to

open our jar and take some sugar out for others, I invite you to look at what you need first. Ask yourself: Should I use my sugar to go to that event or should I use my sugar to repair my internal kitchen? Should I use my sugar for that commitment or should I use my sugar to rest and address my boundaries first?

This is an important distinction because there are many times when we believe that people are taking sugar from us. Yes, some people are taking advantage of us, but outside of abusive relationships, we're allowing them to come inside the kitchen, we're then taking the lid off our jar, and then we're allowing the sugar to be taken. When we choose to continue unhealthy cycles in our relationships, we're allowing them to take our sugar. When we get into the same arguments, especially with people who we know won't change, we're allowing our sugar to be taken. When we say yes even though we really want to say no, we're allowing our sugar to be taken. When we take responsibility for our role in the unhealthy cycle, it doesn't mean that we're solely to blame, BUT it does mean that we can recognize our power and begin to make different choices.

ASK YOURSELF:

- What can my jar actually hold?

- What responsibilities, friendships, relationships, or commitments help me feel more solid and supported?

- Which ones contribute to my feeling drained?

- Have I noticed that certain relationships drain me no matter what?

- What boundaries do I need to put in place to change the amount of sugar going into those relationships?

When you're always showing up as the person who can handle everything, as the person who is "Teflon" to overwhelm, and when you do it all with a smile even though it's quite tough, it drains your sugar jar. Boundaries are a reminder that you can't do it all. And that you teach others how to treat you by teaching yourself how to treat you.

SMALL WAYS TO START SETTING BOUNDARIES

- Saying no even if you're not busy.

- Not promising things that you know you don't want to give.

- Being honest about what you need rather than saying what you think others want to hear.

- Not forcing anything that isn't working (I call this following the natural law of boundaries).

- Saying yes to opportunities that genuinely feel like your worth is understood.

SMALL WAYS TO BEGIN HONORING OTHERS' BOUNDARIES

- Asking people if they're available to talk before calling.

- Asking people what they need from you and honoring it instead of assuming you know.

- Asking people what they're comfortable with, and then doing that.

- Reminding yourself that their boundaries aren't about you.

- Honoring their needs in the same ways you ask people to honor yours.

PROTECT YOUR ENERGY

The whole reason why your sugar is stored inside a jar and the jar is set on a sturdy foundation and kept inside of a safe kitchen with a door that can be locked is so that your energy is protected on multiple levels. For someone to get to your sugar, they'll have to go through multiple steps. The old saying "If you give an inch, they'll take a mile" is super relevant when it comes to boundaries because sometimes people absolutely do this. They think, "Well, I'm in the kitchen, so I might as well go and take a cup of sugar for the road."

This is where your boundaries come in. It can seem harsh to stop someone, but having relationships where you are supported, loved, seen, and feel safe is the minimum. And setting boundaries with others is what will help you feel safe, and the people you're in a relationship with have a responsibility to understand that this is critical to the stability of your relationship. Even though you may care about them, love them, and trust them, it's still important to keep a lid on your jar to protect your energy. You get to decide when they have access, how much they get, and for how long. Keeping a lid on your jar, aka boundaries, is critical to you not over-giving. And sometimes we need to go a step further and close our kitchen door.

SAY NO WHEN YOU MEAN IT

Not only does saying no free us, but it frees other people. Sometimes when we're not honest with others about how we feel, they think that our yes is a FULL, excited yes. Which means they are trusting in our ability to follow through. A part of loving other people is being honest with them about how we feel because we're not doing them any favors by not telling them no. In fact, we could be putting them in a bind because they've stopped looking for their yes now that they believe they've found it in us!

For example, if someone asks if you can help them move and you say yes, they believe you've said yes because you want to. Even if deep down you're exhausted and want to say no, they have no way of knowing that unless you tell them, *even* if they know what's going on in your life and you believe they should know that you're not available. Instead of them continuing their search for help, they've stopped looking because they believe they've found their help in you. If you have to cancel because you realize you really can't follow through with your yes, which should've been a no, they now have a shorter amount of time to find other assistance, which is unfortunate because you knew that you wanted to say no before you said yes. Saying no up front frees both of you. Yes, you're now taking care of yourself by canceling, and life happens sometimes, but you've also put someone you care about in a tough situation when if you'd said no in the first place, they could've found someone else. Sometimes we think we're doing the right thing by saying yes when we mean no, and it's rarely the right thing for anyone involved. Saying yes when we mean no not only hurts our jar, but it impacts others' jars as well.

And even if you toughed it out and showed up for them exhausted, you may not be your full self, and that vibe probably shows. You don't have to be a cheerleader when you're helping others, but it can be very clear that you're doing something you don't want to and that doesn't feel good to either party. Although it can be uncomfortable, being honest and saying no is the best way to take care of yourself and others.

I CAN HAVE BOUNDARIES
AND STILL . . .

- We can love those around us and still have boundaries.

- We can be supportive and still have boundaries.

- We can be parents and still have boundaries.

- We can have romantic partnerships and still have boundaries.

- We can be business owners and still have boundaries.

- We can take care of our parents and still have boundaries.

- We can have deep friendships and still have boundaries.

- We can work hard and give 100 percent and still maintain our boundaries.

There isn't a circumstance where you can't have boundaries. And you get to define them.

Say It with Me

Boundaries keep me from carrying what never belonged to me in the first place.

6

FIND FREEDOM
THROUGH ACCEPTANCE

It was always hard for my friend and me to withhold information from each other when we were face-to-face. Sure, we could do the small-talk "I'm fine" thing through text or on the phone, but not today. Today for a late breakfast we sat down to our baconeggandcheese (one word in NYC) sandwiches with nothing else planned for the day other than catching up. It was that perfect weather where you can feel that summer is handing the baton over to fall and at any minute you'll be reaching for a scarf. I love that time of the year. I looked over at my friend and, with a mouth full of my sandwich, said, "How do you know they're changing this time?"

You know it's an uncomfortable conversation when each person
is taking a bite of food before speaking so that it's clear that it's the
food keeping you from elaborating on the question, not the answer
to the question that's forcing you to think deeper about whether
you believe what you're saying is true.

"I can feel it. After we had that tough conversation, everything just shifted. It's only been a week, but I'm feeling really
positive," she shared while looking down at the sidewalk. "Why
are you looking at me like that," she talked/laughed/ate while
we both broke into a fit of laughter because we knew what each
other was thinking and didn't have to communicate it.

"Nothing, I . . . I really have nothing to say except that I'm
proud of you for having that conversation. And I'm happy things
are shifting. Just give it some time to see if they really mean it this
time . . . " I shared before she abruptly cut me off.

"I thought you had nothing to say," she yelled. We both
laughed again.

I wanted to believe that things were changing for my friend's
relationship. She needed to believe that things were changing
with her relationship because otherwise what was she doing? The
truth was, she was doing the same thing so many of us do. We
hold on to hope that the change we're asking for in our relationships will take place so that we can all be healthier and happier
together. What she wasn't ready to do, what so many of us aren't
ready to do until we absolutely have to, is admit that the person
we love might not want to change, might not have the ability to
change, or is only telling us what we want to hear because, like

us, they don't want to lose the relationship either. When we don't accept the truth, we drain our sugar jars, and each time we deny the truth, the leak grows and grows.

She balled up the foil wrapper to her baconeggandcheese sandwich and stuffed it into the oiled paper bag that held napkins only someone who was looking to get dirtier would use. "How did I get here?" she asked me, not laughing this time. I continued to chew, watching her clean up, as I knew this question wasn't really for me to answer, but for me to listen to. "Do you really think things will change this time? I just want them to be who they say they want to be. I feel like I'm the one pushing for the change, but they're the one who said they want it, you know?"

She was now looking me in the eyes, letting me know I wasn't going to be able to chew myself through these questions as well. "I do believe things will change, if they decide to take the actions that are needed to create the change. You'll have to figure out what you'll need if things continue as they've always been." I stared at my blue-and-white coffee cup that was standard for takeout in NYC. It says, "We Are So Happy to Serve You." *Geez,* I thought to myself. *What a metaphor. When we aren't honest with ourselves, we can't accept what's really happening in our relationships, and therefore we happily serve the version of reality that we want to believe is true or will be true at some point.*

What do we do when we're trying our hardest to let go of the negative energy in our lives, but we find that it also resides in the people, places, and things we love most? Learning to accept the reality of the relationships we have with those we love can be so painful. But it's only through acceptance that we can begin to set ourselves free.

In 2019 I shared a post on Instagram that read:

A part of healing is when you stop relating with people based on who they could be and start accepting who they show up as now.

It's one of the most popular posts I've ever shared and it's because so many of us are in relationships with people we care deeply about based on who we wish they could be rather than who they really are. Sometimes we're in denial, telling ourselves that we see small changes when we really don't. Sometimes we think it's worth it to stick around because we're afraid "someone else will get all of the hard work we put in," when we believe the person may finally change the moment we decide to move on. And other times we believe that loving someone means seeing the best in them, no matter how harmful their behavior may be. When we connect with people based on our desires of what they could be, we're often unable to see how much they're not a match for us in this moment.

Of course, no one is perfect, and people DO change when they WANT to change. A powerful part of acceptance is recognizing that transformation is a personal choice. Growth is a personal choice. Healing is a personal choice. And we can't will change into people's lives without their deciding they want it for themselves because it's up to them to commit to it.

I remember being in a workshop where someone shared, "My

partner is going through a really hard time right now. I'm so sad that this is happening to them, but honestly I hope that *this* is the experience that will finally get them to make the changes I've been asking for." In unison, people around the room said "Mm-hmmm" or "Yup, sometimes that's what it takes." I asked the room, "But what happens if they don't change? I know that sometimes people do live differently after going through hard times and sometimes they don't. What are they communicating, verbally and through their actions to you?"

It's intriguing to think that if the person, relationship, family member, coworker, or friend were to change, then everything would be different for them and thus easier for you. And depending on the situation, that might be true. It's not wrong for you to want someone to improve themselves. It's not wrong for you to desire a healthier connection with the people you love. But it is often harmful to your energy to invest time and attention in any relationship based on the idea of what it could be.

Relationships don't usually go well when they're built on the expectations and hopes that one person has for the other that both of them haven't jointly committed to. The relationship shouldn't be built on who the person could potentially be, even if you do feel they have areas in their life that they can improve. We're often entrusted with being a reflection and a support to the people in our lives; however, we aren't entrusted with ensuring that they choose the decisions that we think are best for them. And not only is it unfair to us to continue in relationships based on what we believe we can convince people to give us, it's also unfair to the person we're in the relationship with because we're constantly measuring them against the expectations that we've set for them, expectations they may not even be interested in meeting.

Seeing the good or potential in people does not mean you can change them or that they want to change.

WHO SAYS THEY NEED THIS CHANGE?

Why are you advocating for this change to occur in their lives? Did they ask you for help? Is this something that would greatly impact their lives? Is there something that they've committed to that's harmful to you or to them and impacts the relationship's ability to survive? Or did you commit to helping them improve their lives without their permission?

Sometimes we feel that by jumping in to help them we're showing them how much we love them. So often we associate love with being able to know what someone needs without their having to ask. Other times we genuinely think we know better than them and we jump in to try to correct their choices. And, of course, there can be many other reasons that we decide to jump in and offer support, but anytime we do this without their permission, unless they're in immediate danger (e.g., pulling them back from walking into the street because they didn't see the car coming), it's a boundary violation, for them and for us.

The person we're attempting to change could be living what

they believe is an incredibly awesome life, and for whatever reason, you want more for them beyond what they want for themselves. Maybe you want to get married when your partner has always made it clear that marriage isn't for them, but you believe you can convince them of something different. Perhaps a friend has made it clear that they don't want that new management position even though you think they would be perfect for it. It's one thing to drop gems in the ears of those you care about so that they can perhaps see a side of themselves that they didn't know existed. This is an amazing thing to do and could lead to their *deciding* to do it for themselves.

But ask yourself: Who says that this change has to occur? Even if you think you're giving them what you believe they really want that they're unable to start on their own, you should be in conversation with them, asking them how you can support them rather than taking on their decisions for yourself. Ensure that they are receptive and would welcome what you're bringing to them.

[NOTE: Sometimes we're trying to help people change because their current choices or behaviors are harmful to themselves and others (e.g., drug or alcohol abuse). I personally know how hard it is to watch someone not choose sobriety, and I completely understand the helplessness that we feel. Even in this situation, we can't force them to choose sobriety, nor can we do the work for them. Ask them how you can support them, but also obtain the help you need through friends, therapists, or a coach to support you in setting healthy boundaries for yourself while you navigate this journey with them.]

THEY DON'T OWE YOU

If they decide to take your advice and help, it's important to be clear with yourself first about what this means. Sometimes we help people because we're doing what we really would love someone to do for us. And so unconsciously we hope that by being a helpful and supportive person in their lives, they'll see how much we care and then provide the same support for us. It's important to mention that this isn't always done out of ill intent or from a malicious or manipulative nature. Sometimes we give from the kindness of our hearts and would also genuinely love it in return someday, and there's nothing wrong with desiring that.

But it's also important to understand who the person is whom you're supporting and to be honest with yourself, about whether their personality or nature has shown you that the way you want them to support you is even possible. Do they recognize the ways that you support them through gratitude? Are they also happy to support you? What would it feel like to support yourself rather than supporting them and hoping for it in return? Is it safe to have a conversation with them and ask for the support you desire? Are there parts of you that don't want to ask because you hope that by depositing love and support all around you people will automatically give this to you in return? How will you feel if the support you provided isn't reciprocated?

It's tough, but unless you were clear on the terms at the beginning of the arrangement the reciprocal support may not happen. For example, after you committed to help them, were you clear that you wanted to be paid money or that they needed to help you in return with a task? The truth is that you may never receive the same level of support or generosity that you've chosen to give. Remember, if it makes you uncomfortable knowing that you may never receive the same thing in return, ask yourself if you should even be signing up to support them in the first place. When we support others, we're using our sugar to do so. And when we don't get that support back, either by someone in our lives or ourselves, that part of our sugar is depleted until we refill it. This can be hard to keep up with if we're constantly depositing our sugar in many places without taking the time to fill our jar back up. It's up to you to decide if you can actually provide that support without feeling upset and it's up to you to decide if you can provide this support while also supporting yourself.

Also, if you do find yourself feeling upset later on or you notice that you have resentment about past times that you've supported others and never received it back, ask yourself: What have I learned about supporting others in the hope that I'll get it in return? What do I need in order to feel comfortable supporting people in my life? How would I have felt if I'd checked in with myself first to see how much energy I had to give before I said yes? How would I have felt if after supporting them for a while, and realizing I was becoming drained, I advocated for myself (with myself) and turned that energy and attention to me? What can I do differently next time or in any situation(s) that I'm in currently?

PAINTING RED FLAGS WHITE

Red flags can be tough to decipher at first because we might tell ourselves that we're overreacting, that we need to get to know them better, or we might make excuses for the red flags to explain them away. When red flags appear, it's our intuition getting our attention. It's up to us to discern whether we agree with the red flags or not. By learning to allow any internal alarm, notification, discomfort, or uneasy feeling to be a sign to pay closer attention to how we're feeling about someone else's behavior, we can begin to learn more about what we need. Red flags don't necessarily mean that the person is "bad" or that they're wrong for us. Red flags are our own intuition setting an alarm off within us that something doesn't feel right. There may be things that are red flags to you that might be completely okay to someone else. It's important to understand what our red flags are and to commit to not comparing or ignoring them with the belief that we should behave like others or that we should bend a bit. When we ignore red flags instead of investigating them, we paint them white and pretend there's nothing going on.

It's important to mention that sometimes we don't know what a red flag feels like because we had harmful experiences where we constantly had to ignore red flags from parents or caretakers. This makes self-trust a challenge, so remember to be kind to yourself as you learn and unlearn. Through denial and sometimes actual inability to be honest with ourselves, we excuse behavior that if we saw it happening to someone else we cared about, we'd immediately recognize it. But it isn't always easy to see what's happening to you, as it's sometimes easier to see it in someone else's life. The cycle may look something like this:

- The relationship starts.

- Red flags begin to pop up within us via our intuition.

- The red flags are telling you to "take a closer look" or "dig deeper" into a specific behavior.

- Our intuition is notifying us that a particular behavior is not in alignment with us. We start communicating back to our intuition (internally with ourselves) that "people can change," "things can shift," and "there's always room for improvement." The red flags are painted white because we've just told our intuition that this alarm was actually a "false alarm."

- We may have a conversation with the other person or a friend that confirms our red flags are valid, but we're not ready to walk away. We believe change is possible. We continue to ignore them.

- Red flags pop up again.

- We paint the red flags white again so that our internal system will stop flagging the same behavior. Because the red flags are now white, there won't be any reason for alarm intellectually, as we've begun to believe that the harmful behavior is okay. We push our intuition away, but emotionally, internally, and spiritually we may still feel uncomfortable.

- We have a conversation with the person we're in the relationship with and they seem to understand what we need. They agree to "try" or they say they "understand," which is great. But we don't walk away with any tangible plan and the uncomfortable situations continue to happen. We also don't recognize any change based on their behavior.

- We've reached the point where we can no longer ignore our discomfort. We commit to trying to get the person to change the very things that were popping up as red flags in the beginning, even though we now have evidence that they aren't interested in change. We reconcile this by remembering that people continue to grow, and perhaps they'll be interested in growing the way we desire them to. We stay in the relationship hoping for change.

[NOTE: Thankfully, people do grow. And there's nothing wrong with asking someone you're in any kind of a relationship with to meet you where you are. But without their commitment to change, via a conversation plus an action, ask yourself: Is change happening?]

Here's an example of the differences between mutually agreed change and the belief that change will happen although there's no evidence of change occurring.

An example of mutually agreed upon change: Tom and Sam are in a relationship and agree to go to therapy to work on communication issues that keep coming up. Sam has been resistant about therapy for some time but has decided that he's ready to go and learn how to communicate better together.

An example of no actionable change: Tom and Sam are having communication issues in their relationship. They often have arguments that are harmful and end without resolution. Tom notices the cycle and asks Sam to go to therapy. Sam says that he'll think about it but never comes back with an answer. Tom is always the one to bring it up again. The cycle continues, and Tom notices that it's getting worse. In the last argument, Tom gave Sam an ultimatum that they go to therapy about the communication issues. Sam says he's sorry and takes Tom on a date as an apology. After the date, Tom is super hopeful that things are changing because he has never seen this side of Sam. Ultimately, Sam still hasn't agreed to go to therapy, and a few days later the communication cycle continues.

Even when we know their behavior is wrong or won't work for us, sometimes we're worried about confronting the other person. Or sometimes we think, "I've made my bed, and now I have to lie in it," which means I chose them and now I should stay—no matter what. Or we don't want to start again, and acknowledging the unhealthy behavior would force us to make decisions that perhaps we're not ready to make.

Ask yourself: Am I listening to my red flags or am I avoiding them? What things am I uncomfortable with that I've noticed in past relationships (romantic or platonic), commitments, careers, or even familial relationships? Are there any behaviors that I know I'm not interested in having in my relationships, such as passive-aggressive or aggressive behavior, harmful language, or unkind gestures, no matter how small? The signs will come from you and red flags are your internal knowledge base of wisdom and experiences you've had with others. Always ask yourself: What am I allowing that's hurting me? What am I allowing that I've already said I was tired of? And then be willing to learn to let it go.

FEAR OF LEAVING PEOPLE BEHIND

As we grow, we may realize that we don't have as much in common with the people in our lives as we used to. This is especially true if you've already committed to your healing journey. I always share this with my new clients. It's unfortunate, but as you embark on your healing journey, you'll sometimes lose people. I, of course, don't want this to happen, but it's often a part of the process because you most likely already have people in your life who are draining you, who aren't a good fit, or who are overwhelmingly unhealthy. And when you start healing, you often make the decision to move on from those relationships once you realize how they don't contribute to your well-being.

When we lose the people who are no longer a good fit, it can leave our communities and circles in a bit of a shock. And so we cherish and want to hold on to the people we still have with everything that we can. And sometimes we fear that our choices (and/or our growth) are pushing us to leave people behind. And this can be scary.

As you know, all relationships are seasonal. Some last for one day, some for months, some for years, and some for a lifetime. And when a separation or space begins from someone we want to keep close, our initial inclination may be to try to convince them to join us on our journey. And it's great to *invite* people to start their own healing journey. It's great to pour into those we love with words of wisdom and affirmation. But it's completely different to begin trying to orchestrate their lives by doing any of the work for them. Or even to get angry with them when they don't follow up with you on the plan that you created for them that they never agreed to.

It's scary to think because you're healing you're outgrowing relationships that you love. It can also be sad and disappointing and come with immense grief. And not every relationship we outgrow will end; sometimes they'll transform into something new. But we set ourselves free when we say yes to our growth and choose ourselves without attempting to bring someone along who isn't interested. Remind yourself that you can *still* love them and have them in your life even if they aren't committed to the same kind of growth as you. And just because you have grown doesn't mean you've outgrown them or that you're on a "different level" than they are. You're just in two different spaces, each living your life as you choose.

HELPING OTHERS HEAL

If you're someone who helps people heal as a coach, a therapist, or a support person, or just someone who feels sensitive to the energy around them, you may feel like it's your calling to help other people figure out their lives. And you may be right that you have a special gift that allows you to help others through incredibly tough things that may be hard for them to go through alone. But just because you can help others heal doesn't mean you should do it without keeping any time for yourself.

As someone in healing work, I know it can be hard sometimes to not jump in and try to help people through the tough problems they have going on in their lives, especially when you believe you see a solution. But it's also important to respect boundaries, with yourself and others, and remember that just because they are your friend or family member it doesn't mean they've hired you as their support. Being a friend, partner, or family member is a different role and commitment than being a healing support in their lives and blurring the line by jumping in to give them un-solicited advice can feel nice and well-intentioned, but it's often a boundary violation for you and others. Ask people what they need from you and resist the urge to provide them with what they haven't asked you for.

THEIR ACTIONS > WHAT THEY SAY

It can be hard to distinguish between the promises or commitments someone makes and their actions when so much of you is invested in the outcome. But it's important to assess what they're doing over what they say they want to do so that you can see if the change is actually taking place. Is their life reflecting the change they want to create? Is their life reflecting the change you both (or the group) committed to? Or have there been a lot of verbal agreements without any actual action?

It's also important to note that emotional expressions can sometimes move us to believe that a person is changing even though there haven't been any actual changes. For example, let's say someone is in a monogamous relationship and they were hurt by their partner having an affair. After talking about it, they both decide to stay in the relationship with the agreement being that there won't be any additional affairs. You will know that they are committed to that agreement based on there not being any other affairs. That is how you measure whether they've taken action or not. Sometimes people try to measure their partner's commitment based on how sorry they appeared to be or how much their partner cried or showed emotion. Although their partner may be legitimately sorry and showed emotion, like crying, for many reasons this is not where the commitment to change stops.

In any circumstance where there has been a commitment, an agreement, or a recommitment, be sure that you are looking at what they're doing, not just what they're saying. This doesn't mean they have to be perfect. This doesn't mean they'll always get it right. But in the example of the affair above, you don't normally slip and fall into bed with someone. The person will have to make choices that keep them from landing in those circumstances.

I remember that at my first job I became friendly with one of my coworkers. Although I liked my job, I knew that I didn't want to be there long. During a fifteen-minute break, I responded to a call for an interview. "I'm so excited about this opportunity, but please don't share this with anyone yet," I said to her. "I really hope you get it because this place kinda sucks," my coworker replied. We both laughed and headed back to work. The next day at lunch in the breakroom, a different coworker walked up to me and in front of everyone at the table said, "So, Yasmine, when are you putting in your notice?" I was so embarrassed and caught off guard. "Ummm . . . I don't know what you're talking about," I replied, staring at the coworker I told the information to in confidence. That person walked away and my coworker confidant and I sat there in a very awkward silence.

What I learned from that experience was not to share anything that I didn't want repeated with people I hadn't built proper trust with. I also eventually shared my disappointment with my coworker, letting her know that I felt betrayed. If I was interested in continuing the relationship, I would've asked that any private information of mine not be shared with anyone unless I'd given permission and that I would do the same for her. Having that conversation would've been a critical part of continuing to build trust. I also took accountability that I willingly shared information that I didn't have to, not from a place of blaming myself, but to acknowledge the entirety of what happened so I could clearly assess what I didn't want to do in the future.

Trust takes time to build and, in both examples shared above, trust was broken. You're not obligated to automatically move forward as if nothing ever happened after trust goes away. It's built back again only with consistent action that allows you to see and understand that you can trust them. And the amount of time it takes varies and can be consistently discussed as time goes on. But you won't know if they've actually changed until they've met the agreement consistently. The important takeaway here is that there is nothing for you to do! You don't have to over-give, or constantly monitor what they're doing, or read their private messages, or listen to their phone calls, or interrogate them regularly. You don't have to add anything to your to-do list to ensure they do what they say they want to do for the relationship. However, if you feel like you need to check their phone, or interrogate them, or pop up on them to see if they're doing what they said, ask yourself: Are we participating in this relationship in a healthy way? Do

I want to be in a relationship where I have to monitor what my partner is doing in order to feel safe? Would I want someone to do these same things to me? With loving honesty, ask yourself if you believe that you'll be able to continue in the relationship without the unhealthy monitoring behavior.

SUPERHERO SYNDROME

Sometimes when a negative thing happens in the lives of people you care about, you may inadvertently feel like it's because you've decided to take a step back. "If I was still showing up for them the way I used to, everything would be okay." We start believing that we can actually save people from their personal choices and that we need to be part of their decision-making process in order for their lives to be okay. Sometimes we're showing up as a savior to others because we're trying to manage our fears and anxiety through them. Our wanting to control them isn't always because we want to control everyone, it's because we want to feel safe.

You may even feel a bit like you have your life "together" more than most and so it's completely fine that you help everyone around you. And it is fine to be supportive to those you love, just not at the expense of yourself or their boundaries. Life has its ups and downs and we can't always control how it manifests in our lives or in the lives of people we care about, and this can be scary. It can make us want to create an atmosphere where we try to ensure that everyone around us is taken care of and we believe that when this happens we'll finally be able to take care of our-selves. But our lives will begin to feel much different when we give ourselves the space to create the safety within without needing to save or control the lives of everyone else.

PEACE AND YOUR SUGAR JAR

In the midst of all the giving, all the fixing, all the showing up, and all the relationships or commitments that you have, there's been a lot of sugar going out and probably not as much going in. We often don't realize how much of ourselves we export in these circumstances because our focus is on how we can help everyone around us. Everyone is able to give at different rates and in different quantities. Remember, everyone has a different-size jar, and every-one may have a different kind of sugar in their jar.

For example, let's imagine someone who prioritizes themselves and has a jar that holds six cups of sugar. Since they're used to op-erating with a fuller jar (because they make themselves a priority), if they become involved in a relationship or commitment that is draining them, they're bound to feel it differently than someone who is used to operating on empty. When we get used to prioritiz-ing ourselves and ensuring that our jars stay full, we're also more likely to discern when we're in a relationship, commitment, or even a conversation that isn't aligned. Prioritizing yourself doesn't mean you won't have relationships where you wish things were different, but it does mean you can show up for yourself despite their choices.

Let's use the same example above, but with someone who struggles with prioritizing themselves and who has the same size jar that holds six cups of sugar. Their jar is already half empty, with three cups of sugar remaining as they head to a conversation with a friend who often leaves them feeling depleted. They might leave feeling depleted for a number of reasons:

- They believe feeling full is based on the friend deciding to change.

- They believe it's their responsibility to fill their friend and hopefully they'll have enough time to fill themselves later.

- They haven't let go of their attachment to their friend's freedom to choose.

- They've tried to find a way to do the work for their friend, depleting the remaining 3 cups of sugar they had left.

We must be willing to decide that someone else's decision about how they want to live their life won't stop us from deciding how we want to live ours. We prioritize our peace by ensuring we aren't putting our lives on hold in the hope that there will be a reward through someone else's life choices. Relationships are rewarding and they provide connection and blessings. We need others and we thrive when we have relationships where we feel safe and seen, so it's understandable that we'd desire to turn those we already love into relationships that meet us. But in doing that, we dedicate ourselves to growth they may not be interested in. Instead, we should focus on how we can dedicate **ourselves** to our peace and our growth, no matter what they decide.

Check in with yourself and ask: Have I ever seen anyone in my life making space for themselves before? What would it feel like to stop taking on "people as projects"? What would it feel like to love or care for people without needing them to change? What would it feel like to love and care for myself without needing others to change?

HOW CAN I FILL MY JAR?

ACCEPT WHO THEY ARE

Sometimes accepting who people are is tough because it can feel like we're giving up on them. And sometimes we feel that if we accept them as they're currently showing up, we're admitting that they're not meeting our needs, which feels "bad" or "wrong" to say about someone we love. But just because someone isn't meeting our needs doesn't mean they're bad. And just because someone isn't interested in being who we're working overtime to get them to be doesn't mean they're bad or lazy or any of those things. Accepting people for who they are sets them free from constantly feeling like they're failing in your eyes because then you get the opportunity to see them for who they are. From there you can choose to love them for the person they are or you can choose to move forward without them.

Accepting people for who they are frees you from using all your energy externally and helps you to save it for yourself internally. You can still do nice things for people. You can still support those you love. You can still be there when things don't go right and they need extra help. You can still surprise them with a gift or an opportunity that's unbelievably thoughtful. But you don't have to dedicate un-limited time and energy to trying to fix problems on their behalf. You don't have to be worried about every decision they make.

When you accept people for who they are, your focus can switch from them to you. You can focus on the things that you've most likely been avoiding in your own life. You can stop talking about other people's problems and start concentrating on how to get the things you desire. And you can release the pressure that you have on yourself (and on others) to do anything but live life exactly as you choose.

MINDING YOUR BUSINESS

Sometimes the main thing that we don't know how to do is how to mind our business. We don't have to be involved in everything that everyone has going on in their lives. We don't have to offer advice on every decision that others make. You are not Chip and Joanna on the *Fixer Upper* version of relationships. It's not your job to upgrade everyone else's kitchen. And everyone's life doesn't need to be "upgraded" because some people are living their best life without your comments and opinions!

What would it feel like to answer the questions you receive from friends and family and not turn those questions into a three-hour research project for yourself? What would it feel like to show up and support those in your life with only the time that you actually have available and not always from a place of over-giving? What would it feel like to exercise your boundaries in external relationships by reminding yourself that your time matters, too?

Reminding yourself that not everything is your business can be incredibly helpful to staying in your lane. It can be hard to let go, but releasing this hold on people and things that don't actually belong to you can free you.

Say It with Me

When I let go of others, I have space to hold on tighter to me.

When I listen to my intuition, I'm led to what is aligned for me.

I am ready for healthy relationships where I am met with reciprocity, ease, and fun.

7

LETTING GO AS A
SELF-CARE PRACTICE

About ten years ago I decided I was finally ready to start blogging and sharing my writing. Even though I didn't feel confident enough to call myself a writer at that time, this felt like a good first step and I was keeping a promise that I'd made to myself to try putting myself out there. It was also great timing to intentionally have something to work on that was bringing new creative energy into my daily life, as I'd just moved into my own place with my daughter after separating from her dad.

I was in a college at the time, and our first class instruction was to share something that we were working on that we were excited about while also giving constructive feedback to one another. Although blogging wasn't my business, it did feel like an opportunity to share my writing and hear what others thought. I shared my blog link and moved on to begin writing feedback on other people's posts. Suddenly, I started receiving notifications that people were responding to my blog. Excitedly, I clicked onto the page where I could read their feedback, and I was stunned.

Post after post tore everything that I wrote apart. One woman shared feedback with me that I can clearly remember as if it just happened. It said: "Yasmine, this may sound harsh but I'm hoping this can save you a lot of time. You're not a good writer, and there's nothing captivating about anything that you say. Please, find something else to do as I'm sure you have some other talent—as this is not it. Said with love." This *Game of Thrones*–style public shaming was one of the most hurtful experiences I'd ever had on my creative work. A huge part of me was like "Yasmine, they're trying to be helpful! This is going to help you grow," which is BS because you don't have to be hurtful to help people, something I was still learning. Another part of me was like "F**k these people and their feedback!" But there wasn't any part of me that was ready to see what I needed in that moment, and instead of offering myself forgiveness for the typos or other feedback they shared with me, I joined the "Who do you think you are?" train and tore myself apart.

To be honest, self-forgiveness wasn't even a viable option because I didn't even know we could forgive ourselves. I thought my focus was on being self-accountable and responsible, but the internal chatter often sounded a lot like judgment and negative self-talk. Instead of forgiving myself for any typos or grammatical errors, I was hard on myself and said, "If you'd done a *better job* of proofreading, then this wouldn't have happened." Once I moved past the typos, instead of forgiving myself for sharing my work with a group of people, which wasn't safe for helpful feedback, I said to myself, "You've got to learn how to be a *better* judge of character, and maybe get a thicker skin."

These same struggles with forgiveness spilled over into other areas of my life as well. If I accidentally hurt a friend, I beat myself up for days even after I'd apologized because I believed my mistake was evidence that I was flawed. If a romantic partner cheated on me, I focused more on why I couldn't forgive them and move on instead of my own emotions, feelings, and needs. I thought about whether the cheating occurred because I wasn't doing enough in the relationship and I would blame myself for choosing a relationship where I was even dealing with these circumstances. The self-blame was tenfold. Self-demeaning comments like "You're always making mistakes, get it together" or self-inquiries like "What is wrong with you" worsened the problem.

In every area of my life, if anything occurred, I thought about what I *could* or *should* have done to prevent it and rarely let myself off the hook for being a normal person who was living and learning. Instead, every instance of self-perceived error made me evaluate, consciously and unconsciously, whether I belonged in the spaces and with the people I had around me.

Over time, my perfectionism and lack of self-worth became a barrier to what I thought it would give me access to. I thought always saying the right things would ensure that I belonged. I thought that never making mistakes would ensure a happy and successful life. And I had success, but I was rarely able to enjoy it or rejoice in it because I was always worried about what mistakes might be coming the moment I took my eye off perfectionism and *gasp* spent time having fun. I was always wondering when people would find out that I wasn't as worthy as they thought.

It may sound like I'm talking more about worthiness than forgiveness, but I often find that it's hard for us to even imagine forgiving ourselves if we don't first learn to believe in our worth. We're more likely to extend forgiveness or excuses to others, even those who've been harmful to us, and withhold it from ourselves when we believe we must earn our worthiness. And it's completely okay to forgive others for whatever you choose, as forgiveness is your decision. But it's also important that we learn how we can give that same courtesy to ourselves.

Although I didn't know it when I submitted that blog for feedback, I'd unconsciously set the bar pretty high for my expectations on what they'd say, as I did often. And although the feedback I received was truly unacceptable, I didn't create any space for making mistakes and to naturally not always get it right sometimes. At this time, my self-worth was strongly tied to what I did and what I produced. And the feedback that I'd received for quality work was what filled me up until the next "project" arrived. Being excellent at my job was what kept me going and I believed that this was a healthy way to strive because it was helping my career. But in reality, this unhealthy striving or perfectionism put me in a position where even when I was being harmed, like I was during that "constructive" feedback session on my blog, instead of being on my own side, I joined them in responding to their harmful comments about my writing with

"You're right, I should really work on my grammar" or "This was my first blog post, and you're right I should've waited until I was more experienced to share this." I thought by responding to their harmful feedback I was being professional. I thought I was taking the higher road and that this was growth. This wasn't growth, though; it was self-harm. And I had to learn to love myself through the embarrassment of later realizing I cosigned their harmful behavior.

Perfectionism, lack of self-worth, and working to earn your worth are often responses to experiences we've had growing up or even as adults that told us this is how you stay safe, stay seen, and get love. We unconsciously begin behaving this way, with ourselves and others, and repeat harmful language to ourselves as a damaging form of motivation. We may also struggle with receiving praise and find it hard to believe that we deserve it because our focus is on being better next time. There is very little room for self-forgiveness when we're in this cycle. Self-forgiveness allows you to say to yourself, "Of course I can do a better job next time! It's okay I made some mistakes, I'm human. But let's take a second and talk about how great this time went? I'm so proud of me."

Forgiveness often invites us to explore acceptance, and for so many of us, we fear that acceptance translates to agreement and we don't often want to admit or agree to things that feel uncomfortable, to mistakes we've made, and we don't want to agree with harmful things that have happened to us. For example, when I agreed with the harmful comments that were made about my blog post because I thought I was taking the high road, I didn't do it because I agreed with them or because I wanted those comments. I did it because I thought that agreeing with them was the *professional* and *right* thing to do. This wasn't agreement, this was telling them they were right in the hopes that it would stop the attacks because they'd see my "true" character for wanting to get it right. In reality, this was not helpful to me or for the situation.

Acceptance doesn't mean encouraging more harmful behavior or welcoming more mistakes. It means embracing what took place with clarity and empathy, while being honest with yourself about what hurt. This helps us move toward the step of seeing who we are during our mistakes and loving ourselves anyway. And this helps us move into the practice of forgiving ourselves. Sometimes, the choices we've made, especially the ones that didn't work, help us to learn what does work.

To learn more about ourselves beyond what we've been told we need to make those major or minor missteps so that we know what we want and gain clarity about what we don't want. The growth we seek is in taking risks, and the risks come with the potential of what we perceive as a win or a loss, but either one teaches us a lesson. When placed in that same situation of sharing my first blog post, while armed with self-forgiveness, self-worth, and self-trust, I *still* wouldn't be able to change the way they were choosing to respond to me. I could, of course, advocate for myself, but that also doesn't necessarily mean they'd be any kinder. But what would be different is the way I would respond to myself about their feedback. I could acknowledge that I was hurt and walk myself through that tough experience while *still* believing that writing was for me, no matter what they thought. What could also be made clear is that I wasn't interested in hearing hurtful feedback of any kind. Constructive feedback never has to be what I experienced that day. I could give myself the grace of recognizing that I was obviously sharing with a crowd that was not my people. And this is what grace embodies, being willing to give ourselves space to figure out our truth.

A part of healing is making space for mistakes. When you believe that you always have to get it right, you preserve the idea that there is a right way. And you may even be hard on yourself for not doing it the right way when in truth there is no evidence of what the right way is. You get to define for yourself what "right" means. You may think being tough on yourself will help you persevere when the cycle is really one of you upholding a standard of rightness that is unclear, even to you. The standard is you constantly moving the goalpost around and creating space to consistently tear yourself down.

It's important to understand that you're going to make decisions in your life that felt good at one point. You crossed all your *t*'s and dotted all your *i*'s as best as you could and thought for sure this was a sound choice. And over time, what felt sound, safe, and sure based on the experience you had in that moment turns out to have consequences, emotions, and work involved that you couldn't have foreseen. In those moments, we might turn to ourselves and ask, "What the hell was I thinking?" But making choices that you later find you no longer want is a part of life. Understanding that you want to change your mind is evidence that you're tapped into your knowing. You're listening to your intuition. You're not just moving through life unattached to your desire—which is a sign of your immense dedication to yourself. But also we often make new decisions when that feeling of discomfort comes up. It's like the yield sign that lets you know it's time to slow down and see what's up. All of this is a part of growth and something you should celebrate being attuned to.

Putting the expectation on yourself to be in "perfect" form as you move through tough decisions or uncomfortable emotions is often unrealistic. And it's a learned behavior, which is good news because it means you can unlearn it even though it might be tough and take time. It's normal to have anger. It's normal to have sadness. And sometimes you may even lose your temper. You won't always be able to respond to yourself or others in a measured way. And depending on what you're dealing with, responding with anger MAY be the most grounded response. Society has a tendency to ask women, femmes, Black people, and POC to respond to upsetting circumstances with charm and ease. This is a perpetuation of oppressive and unhealthy cycles that we are absolutely charged to move against. There is nothing wrong with anger; there is nothing wrong with displaying it. And anger doesn't have to be disrespectful or harmful. But it is a part of being human.

Healing doesn't make you a robot. There's a misconception that healing will remove all of your tendencies to curse, tell someone about themselves, gossip . . . and the list goes on. Healing doesn't make you a perfect version of yourself; it helps you gain more clarity about who you are, what you want, and what you need to do to get there. Forgiving yourself for when you made decisions that unfortunately negatively impacted your time, your body, or your life IS a part of healing. You will always be human and therefore this practice of forgiveness for yourself and others will ALWAYS be needed.

It's also important to know that everything isn't your fault. There are things that will happen to you that you absolutely have zero control over. You couldn't have known, when choosing a particular job, for example, that the boss you loved would leave a month after you'd gotten there and be replaced by someone who is incredibly hard to deal with. Sometimes things go awry and even in the circumstances where you may believe that you "brought this on yourself" you deserve care, love, compassion, and to be seen. And you deserve self-forgiveness. Because being hard on yourself will not cause the situation to undo itself. But looking at yourself with kindness can help you heal and soften you enough to begin to take next steps.

Even though the people in that class were being hard on me, they didn't come close to how hard I was being on myself. A few days after the blog comments, a few women direct-messaged me and said they were so sorry to see what was happening and checked in to see if I was okay, while offering support for whatever I needed. I remember thinking how kind that was and wondering what it would be like to do that for myself. It was the first time that I realized I could *choose* to be kind to myself, even in moments when I was sure it was my fault. I realized that my negative self-talk was unkind, and I also realized that the internal negative self-talk wasn't my truth. My negative self-talk was often other people's statements toward me replayed internally in my voice as truth, at the most opportune times. I recognized that I could continue to beat myself up, much like those commenters were doing to me in the name of "constructive criticism." Or I could practice self-compassion, self-love, and a completely new concept to me: self-forgiveness.

My first step was accepting the offers of support from two of the women who reached out, one of whom I'm still friends with today. This helped me begin to remove the stories that I had about having to figure out my feelings alone. Although self-forgiveness was still my personal choice and my work to do, I could accept and receive help along the way. Next, I deleted my comments that appeared to support the harmful feedback. This helped reinforce within me that it was never too late to be on my side. I continued to write, and although I was nervous to share my writing publicly again for years, I kept working at it just for me until I was ready to share it again. Then I began working on forgiving myself for being hard on myself, for abandoning myself, for betraying myself, and for being ashamed. I reminded myself that forgiveness might take time and that I would be there for myself even if I found myself in this harmful cycle again. I reinforced to myself that I wasn't going anywhere.

Through practicing self-compassion, I learned that the language I use internally doesn't have to be final. Everything I say to myself is written in pencil as far as I'm concerned. When I decide that what I've said isn't working or I realize that what I've said to myself is harmful, I can erase it and rewrite it with a new clarity that allows for peace, joy, and understanding to exist. When I work with clients or in group settings, I always like to remind them that their mind can sometimes be like our TV's DVR device that records everything we've done and at just the right time it likes to pull out the video that has similarities to what we're currently going through as evidence for us to review. And in those moments, instead of using that evidence as proof of our failures, we can decide to see ourselves as doing what we thought would work out and evidence of our ability to keep trying rather than evidence of us not getting it right. And then you change the channel or delete the recording when you realize it's no longer relevant to what you need. You can always remind yourself of what's helpful or what isn't. And self-forgiveness asks us to be the biggest advocates we can for ourselves.

WORTHINESS

If someone asked me if there were any necessary pillars of healing, worthiness would absolutely be one of them. Worthiness often translates into wanting to feel like we deserve to belong, and often there's an internal debate taking place where we're hoping to have our worthiness confirmed through others. Some people will show up in our lives and tell us how worthy they believe we are. And there's nothing wrong with being validated by our friends, family, partner, coworkers, and even our boss. It's completely fulfilling and necessary to have people in your life who will honestly and consistently cheer you on. This is a beautiful thing to have in all of your relationships. But unfortunately, it doesn't contribute to filling us up if we don't also believe what they're saying about ourselves as well.

For some of us, somewhere along the line of our lives, we experienced situations that made us feel we weren't deserving. Perhaps we were teased or bullied in school, maybe we had family members who were mean or harmful to us, or perhaps it was just society around us constantly pushing images of what they believed deserving people looked like—and we didn't think we measured up. It's truly unbelievable how young we are when we begin to piece together who we think is valued and how we believe we measure up to them.

Belonging helps us feel secure and seen, but if we are performing to belong, then we don't actually belong at all. If we have to be anything other than ourselves to fit in, then the space wasn't made for us. And even if we have a place in this group, deep down we know it isn't organic and therefore it doesn't truly work. And all of this can contribute to and come from a lack of worthiness that we feel innately belongs to us.

You can also struggle with worthiness because of things that have happened to you as an adult, like losing your job and having to start over, a relationship ending, a ton of stress that feels tough to keep up with, familial issues where you don't feel like you belong in your family, or any abusive situation. When worthiness is a struggle, we're harder on ourselves (with or without perfectionism), and we're more likely to continue harmful cycles in our lives and relationships because it's hard to choose yourself when you're waiting for the belonging to happen outside yourself.

All of the situations above need the salve of self-forgiveness.

ASK YOURSELF:

- Where do I struggle with worthiness (e.g., romantic relationships, career, friendships, etc.)?

- When do I tend to be hard on myself?

- Was anyone in particular hard on me when I was growing up or in specific relationships?

- Are there any places or spaces where I feel pressure to belong?

- When do I feel easefully worthy? What am I doing and whom am I with when I find it easier to believe in my innate worthiness?

SELF-FORGIVENESS AS A PRACTICE

Self-forgiveness is where we learn to accept our humanness. We don't actually *need* to work on any part of who we are; we get to choose what we want to change, so self-forgiveness also allows us to remove the urgency that we sometimes place on ourselves to get things done by a certain time frame or age. It asks us to allow any admission of mistakes and to gracefully work through our choices. Self-forgiveness asks us to use our internal voice with gentleness and to understand that it may take time for any form of balance we're seeking to manifest in our lives. Self-forgiveness asks you for the chance to grant any mistakes the ease of being lessons so that they can be absorbed into you as wisdom.

When we've violated our own boundaries, the boundaries of others, or something has taken place that makes us feel insecure, it can be hard to practice self-forgiveness immediately because we've lost our sense of safety. Practicing self-forgiveness often starts with calming yourself down through grounding techniques, like meditation, taking a walk in nature, or speaking with a therapist or friend who can hold space for you. Also, take this time to admit to yourself what you're disappointed by, what's hard to accept, or what feels heavy. Make space for your self-forgiveness practice to allow you to hold both the tough parts of your experience and the compassion you deserve.

Practicing self-forgiveness can also look like writing or reciting affirmations like these:

- I forgive myself for the moments when I didn't mind my business.

- I forgive myself for the times I violated my own boundaries.

- I forgive myself for bringing people into my life who drained me.

- I forgive myself for staying longer than was good for me.

- I forgive myself for quitting when I was afraid.

- I forgive myself for not going through with my dreams because I was afraid.

- I forgive myself for trying to carry it all alone.

- I forgive myself for . . .

Practicing self-forgiveness can also look like writing notes or reciting audio notes to yourself like this:

"*Honestly, I'm so upset that I didn't see this coming. I've had situations before where I've received harsh constructive criticism, but this time hurt so badly.* But what I do know **is that this time I at least realized what was happening,** *even if I was unable to stop it before it happened.* **I saw the cycle playing out and now at least I know what it is, and that's growth.** *Every time I catch myself being hard on myself,* **I'm going to remind myself that this time WAS different. I'm slowly making the change I'm seeking** *and this is amazing even though it's still tough.* **And I forgive myself for being in this situation again because now that I see the cycle I know that I really didn't know what I was getting myself into before.** *But now at least* **I can be there for myself by trying to shift what I can** *to make sure it doesn't happen in a way that brings me discomfort or harm in the future.* **And if I find myself in a similar situation in the future, I will be there for myself again.**"

There is both honesty and gentleness in this note. Self-forgiveness doesn't mean a lack of self-accountability. But it also doesn't mean you have to devalue yourself. There may be shame present and you have the opportunity to acknowledge it with kindness and perhaps share it with someone you can trust, including yourself. Anytime you allow vulnerability to override "toughing it out" or "suffering silently," you choose self-forgiveness. Self-forgiveness is limitless and we can choose to practice self-forgiveness as often as we need to.

FORGIVENESS OF OTHERS

Do you find that you're able to forgive others easier than you're able to forgive yourself? Do you find that forgiveness of others helps you move on? Do you find forgiveness of others almost impossible? Do you feel that forgiveness of others implies weakness? Or do you find that forgiveness in your relationships rarely comes up?

None of these are right or wrong, but they provide a starting place of self-inquiry to get curious about the way you look at forgiveness, how it impacts the way you relate to others in relationships, and of course how it impacts the way you look at yourself. Sometimes when discussing forgiveness the focus is heavily placed on how it looks with the people who hurt you, which is of course important. But that places your full focus on others, which doesn't shift or change your energy within.

With every client that I've worked with one-on-one or in any workshop that I've ever facilitated, we always end up talking about forgiveness, even if it's not a topic that's scheduled to be discussed, because people want to understand why it's hard for them to move forward or why something feels so heavy so many years later. Or perhaps they've realized that they don't believe they'll be able to forgive someone and they're nervous that it may impact the way they heal or they wonder, "Does this mean I'm not healing correctly?" The truth is, we can only take the healing steps that we're ready to take and deciding not to take a particular healing path doesn't mean we're doing anything wrong.

A big part of being able to forgive others relies on understanding our part in it (if any), understanding how we feel about what we believe was done to us, reconciling with the part of ourselves that may find it hard to accept what happened, determining if any boundaries need to be put in place to protect us from behavior like this in the future, and ultimately asking ourselves if we actually want to forgive. Forgiveness is not automatic because even if we're forgiving someone else, forgiveness is really for us.

It doesn't mean that if someone has done something that you find hard to forgive that you're doing it wrong if you don't forgive them. Forgiveness toward others is an option that you have. Even if you truly care about someone, you can still decide that something they've done is unforgivable based on your definition of what forgiveness is. And when I say forgiveness is really for you, it means that the act of forgiving only impacts your sugar jar. Yes, it may relieve the person whom you've chosen to forgive, but forgiveness is not an energy exchange. Forgiveness is often a release of energy within you.

Thinking again about your sugar jar, think about a time in real life where you were using a spoon to get some sugar out of a jar. Sometimes you'll find clumps of sugar in the jar and you may not know how they got there. If you were baking or doing something where you wanted the exact measurement, you'd break up those clumps of sugar before using it because when sugar is in a clump it could be a lot or a little, we don't actually know how much. But we do know that it takes up space in the jar and the sugar doesn't flow as easily.

When you're holding a grudge or when there's anger, disappointment, or even fear inside of you, you're bound to get those clumps of sugar in your jar. And to be clear, there's nothing wrong with having some clumps in your jar—no matter how big or small. We're not here to spend all of our time unearthing every single thing we've ever been through to have the perfect jar with the perfect sugar.

We're here to hopefully live a full life enjoying it as much as we can. But if a situation occurs where we decide to forgive someone, that clump of sugar in our jar is released. Why? Because we release the energy that we've been holding on to. It doesn't mean that they have to come back into your life if you've set a boundary that the relationship is over. Your forgiving them doesn't mean that they were right and you were wrong. Your forgiving them doesn't mean you're letting them off the hook. Forgiveness is a form of letting go and releasing emotions that you're holding against certain people or situations. And that provides more ease for you, more space for you, and more internal freedom for you. Forgiveness moves the energy within you, and you won't honestly know how it impacts someone else unless they decide to share it with us.

Forgiveness also doesn't mean that you must go on as if the incident or experience never happened. Forgiveness is not the tool from *Men in Black*. It doesn't completely erase everyone's memories, although so many wish it did. And telling yourself not to think about it anymore doesn't work either, it just makes us feel like we're doing something bad by bringing our attention to something that needs it. Forgiveness takes patience and often an undetermined amount of time. Understanding that your decision to forgive still leaves room for you to have more questions or to want to have more conversations about the situation, as needed, may be a boundary you'd like to explore before you decide whether you're ready to forgive.

Also, it's helpful to understand that receiving an apology for a behavior, an incident, or a circumstance that was harmful may not "cure" all of our feelings as we've often been taught saying "I'm sorry" does. Yes, hearing that someone is apologetic for what they've done can be a start to deciding whether you'd like to explore forgiveness, but the true essence of apologizing is realized through action and therefore often takes time. Allow yourself to get curious about what "sorry" means to you and how you can redefine it in a way that allows you to accept an apology while still being present to what you'll need in addition to the words. And, of course, this goes both ways in relationships.

REPAIRING YOUR SUGAR JAR

When we struggle with practicing self-forgiveness, our jar may have cracks in it, making way for a steady stream of sugar that's consistently being lost. It takes a lot of energy to focus on our mistakes or errors, it takes a lot of energy to practice perfectionism, and it takes a lot of energy to consistently tear yourself down. When it's tough to practice self-forgiveness, we're usually also struggling with taking care of ourselves, and that means our jars aren't being replenished regularly.

Now, people will always be excited to come into your kitchen and check out your sugar jar when they realize you've got some tea. It's hard to hide a trail of sugar leaking from your jar. It shows up in your actions and for some of us on our faces as we wear how we're feeling there, and sometimes our connections with others are built on shared unhappiness. For some, hearing how you're not doing well helps them compare and feel better about themselves and some people just love the "excitement" of hearing someone else's story. You can tell the difference between those who are there to hold you and those who are there with their cup ready.

Statements like "Oohh, this is a good story" or displayed excitement while you're sharing pain is usually evidence that you're probably not talking to the right people in those vulnerable moments. The people you choose to support you in these tender moments will affect how your sugar jar reacts. I mention this because self-forgiveness can be harder when the people around us aren't there to help; they've arrived to gossip. Recognizing who isn't helpful to your progress is often the first step so that you can deny them entry to your kitchen and gain back control over the atmosphere around your jar.

ASK YOURSELF:

- Are the people who normally show up to support me actually providing me with support?

- What do I always wish I had when leaving conversations?

- What would be helpful to hear when I'm being hard on myself about something that happened?

Next, let's look at how we can begin repairing your jar. This may take time, but the work will enrich you so much because it'll help stop a drain of energy that isn't allowing you to feel full. We want to work on redefining the way you look at yourself when things don't go the way you wanted them to, and change the language you use to talk to yourself.

ASK YOURSELF:

- How do I currently look at my mistakes?

- How do I feel about where I am in my life right now?

- What are the things I enjoy about my life?

- What are the things I'd like to change or shift?

- How have some of the mistakes I've made helped me to do the things I now enjoy?

- How have some of the mistakes I've made taught me what to do or say when confronted with things that don't align?

- How do I feel about my wisdom?

- How have I grown this year?

Now, looking at where you've been and where you are now, name three things that you're proud you've done for yourself. Be sure to put these someplace where you can regularly look at them and remind yourself of what you've already done for you. Or you can dog-ear this page.

Examples of things you could be proud of:

- Buying this book and committing to these exercises, which is impacting your healing and life.

- Choosing yourself.

- Setting tough boundaries.

- Making space for fun/joy.

- Meeting a goal that you set for yourself.

This part of the exercise plugs up the cracks in your jar. Continue to remind yourself of what you've done for you and how you continue to commit to you and the repairs will get stronger and stronger. And don't worry, if you continue to struggle you can always come back to this discussion. This is why we call it practice.

Lastly, now that we've repaired the jar, we want to fill it with some actions and affirmations.

Options for actions:

- Connect with a friend and tell them about something you're proud of yourself for.

- Think about a compliment or an affirmation that you've received that was hard to let in at the time, and make space to receive it within now.

- Write a list or recite an audio note of how self-forgiveness is changing the way you look at yourself. (If it's still tough to practice self-forgiveness, you can change this action to talking about how you are looking forward to self-forgiveness changing the way you look at yourself.)

- Make time to celebrate yourself in small ways when you choose self-forgiveness. Bonus: Create a celebration list that you can turn to when you're ready to celebrate!

Let the feelings of disappointment flow. Don't turn away from them, don't try to hide them, and don't stuff them down. Cry if you need to, take the day off—do whatever it is you need to in order to take care of yourself. Once you've allowed yourself to feel those feelings, choose one of the options above to help you bring some joy back in. We can hold space for joy while processing the tough stuff.

Say It with Me

I can feel more than one feeling at the same time. Practicing self-forgiveness allows me to hold myself with empathy while recognizing my discomfort.

I knew I was healing when I was able to see my mistakes as growth opportunities.

When I decide to forgive others, the forgiveness is for me.

8

HEALING AS THE PARENT
AND AS THE CHILD

NOTE: While this chapter talks about parenting, I also intentionally share a story that incorporates emotions that so many of us experience whether we're parents or not, emotions like grief, trauma, fear, depression, and even loneliness. Most of us have experienced being parented by someone, the good and the tough parts, and what unites us is the desire we often have to find ways to reparent ourselves as we learn more about what we need now based on what in retrospect we didn't receive then. If you've decided you don't want to be a parent, or you're a foster parent, or you're a caretaker, or you've adopted, I also talk about healing from those perspectives as well. I hope this chapter invites you to learn more about how parenting affects your healing journey and how you can incorporate new ways of being there for yourself by revisiting your experiences around parenting as a whole.

While resting after fifteen hours of labor and delivery to a healthy six pounds, nine ounces baby girl, I woke up, overhearing a whispered conversation between a nurse and my daughter's dad as they talked about her condition. The nurse shared, "Your baby has stopped breathing two times from what appears to be apnea and is also having seizures. We're mobilizing transport to take her to the nearest neonatal intensive care unit (NICU) in Albany, Georgia, which is almost two hours away." I jumped out of bed, ran to see my daughter, and walked in on her receiving CPR. I completely lost any sense of reality. I fell to the floor screaming. I didn't know what to do in that moment and was completely shattered at what was happening to her. And then, about five minutes later, I jumped into action mode. I started packed my things, saying, "I'm going with her, there's no way I'm leaving her alone." They replied, "Ma'am, you aren't authorized to leave the hospital, it hasn't been twenty-four hours since you've given birth." I responded, "Unless you are going to have me arrested, I'm packing my things and I'm driving to meet my child."

People were running around; there was shouting and crying. It was frantic. My doctor, whom I'd seen for the last nine months, kept trying to encourage me to stay just a bit longer as they knew

I was weak, but I refused. My doctor told me, "I won't be able to give you anything for the pain," which I found odd at the time because I hadn't asked for anything. At that moment, nothing mattered but trying to get to my daughter as soon as I could. We weren't allowed to leave the hospital with her and it was illegal to follow the ambulance by car, so after she left we braced ourselves at the door. I'll never forget leaving that hospital with my daughter's father and my doctor grabbing me and giving me something to take, because in that moment she could still give me pain meds. She said, "You can't feel the pain you're in now, because your adrenaline is running, but when it wears off, hopefully this will help you."

We spent twelve of the longest and scariest days of my life in the NICU with her. The first few days were the hardest as we watched her fight for her life, contemplating whether we'd have to put her on a ventilator. We hadn't had any actual sleep since the evening before I went into active labor. I remember a hospital security guard, who I suppose had watched me walk around the hospital all night and all day, stopped me and said, "Baby, there is nothing else that you can do today. You've got to go home and rest." She was right; I could barely walk without excruciating pain. My breasts were completely swollen and in pain as I hadn't been able to feed her since she'd been born. Because I'd checked myself out of the hospital to be with her about eight hours after giving birth, I didn't get the chance to meet with any of the doctors you normally talk to before you check out, so I didn't know how to pump, breastfeed, or take care of my body.

I didn't understand any of the things that I would've learned about if we'd been discharged normally. Luckily, the NICU doctors helped me with this, providing me with a pump, and thank goodness, I'd overpacked my hospital bag with all the things you think you'll never need. I was able to pump at the local hotel we'd checked into and lived at until she was able to leave twelve days later.

We were only able to visit three times a day for about fifteen to twenty minutes at a time to minimize germs those first few days. I'll never forget on the fourth day after scrubbing up we walked into the room and the doctor said, "She's actually doing pretty good today. No seizures or apnea episodes so far, but I wouldn't get too excited . . ." but whatever else he mentioned trailed off because WE KNEW she was healed. We just did. The next time we visited she could eat. The time after that, she didn't need oxygen. And the next time we visited the NICU, they told us she'd been moved to the nursery as she was no longer critical. The day we were finally able to take her home felt like the heaviest and lightest day all in one. It was a relief, but I was also terribly nervous to take home this baby, without experience, who'd just been through so much.

For me, parenthood began in a traumatic way that I recognize not a lot of people experience. My pregnancy and childbirth already presented some trauma to my body and was a life-changing experience in itself. Combined with everything that took place, I could've never imagined that would happen to my baby. That was my first true introduction to recognizing that sometimes life will happen no matter how much you plan for it. You can't always be prepared for the things that come your way because you won't always know what's coming. Being a caretaker to others is a big introduction to wanting to do the best you can but it also means not having full control of all the potential outcomes. It's balancing letting go with faith like I never thought was possible while still holding on as tightly as I could.

Whether you're a parent right now, interested in having kids in the future, or not interested in parenting at all, we've all had moments in our lives when we encountered traumatic experiences that we never saw coming. We've all had moments when we felt helpless to what was happening around us. We've all had moments when we knew we'd have to trust that things would be okay, because we weren't going to be able to impact whether things would actually be okay. We may have been children or adults during these experiences, but we knew in those moments that we'd changed, even if we didn't yet know how. Whether you experience post-traumatic stress or post-traumatic growth, or both, trauma can change the way we interact with the world around us.

In the midst of my gratitude of recognizing my daughter was going to be okay and adjusting to motherhood overall, I began experiencing postpartum depression. I wouldn't know for years that I'd experienced it, as it wasn't until I looked back and processed it that I knew what happened to me. I was completely ashamed to talk about it as I felt like I'd be complaining when I'd just been given the gift of being able to come home with my daughter. I also blamed myself for what happened to her, even though we knew that it was nothing that I did or that anyone had done to create her condition. And so with the immense shame that I felt about sharing what I'd just gone through, I kept it from everyone, which added to my feelings of loneliness. I tried moving on with life as if nothing had happened, which of course did not make things easier. And four months after her birth, her dad deployed for a year, so I was left figuring out how to manage my emotions, motherhood, and everything else on my own.

You might be wondering why this parenthood chapter is talking about trauma as generally chapters like it talk about the magic of parenthood. And, listen, I am grateful to be a mom and I absolutely love my kids and I feel honored to be their person. But I also felt encouraged to talk about the many layers of trauma I experienced during something that is painted as a primarily joyful time. For people who become parents through pregnancy, that road sometimes includes loss before you get there. My first miscarriage was completely shocking because I remember thinking that I didn't know anyone this had happened to. And it wasn't until it happened to me that the women around me shared that it had also happened to them. I realized then that it was happening to so many of us and we were most likely suffering silently. Throughout life, many of us have decided not to share the tough parts because it feels like they are only happening to us.

During my pregnancies I also experienced so much racism in the medical system, which was also traumatic. I couldn't always trust that my providers were really listening to my concerns. In both of my pregnancies, I had to change doctors multiple times until I found someone who would listen to me. Whether your child comes to you through pregnancy, adoption, fostering, surrogacy, or any of the other wonderful ways we get to be parents today not being heard regularly is also a traumatic experience that we don't often address or discuss. And if you're not parenting, the theme of not being heard or listened to has most likely touched you as well.

Although parenthood doesn't always start in such a traumatic way for all of us, and thank goodness it doesn't, we still may come to adulthood potentially carrying the unresolved past traumas we've experienced, which definitely impacts the way we choose to parent or be in relationship with others. There's usually a moment when we become a parent where we realize that it is going to require way more than just providing the basics like clothing, food, and shelter. This commitment may require us to become a different version of ourselves. This commitment may require us to do things we said we'd never do. This commitment may require parts of us we've never used before or that we've never seen in anyone else. And this isn't what society shares with us when we're taught about parenting. And even though we know society isn't where we should get all our wisdom from, sometimes it's all we know or all we have access to.

When we experience trauma, we sometimes think about what we would have done differently if we'd known then what we do now. I remember thinking that if I could go back, I would've talked to more people about the pain I was experiencing, especially my grandmother. I don't know what she could've offered me in those moments, but mostly I wished I hadn't held back telling her or others because of my fear and shame. Being a parent now, I know that she worried anyway. Being a parent now, I know that she was concerned anyway. I also wish I'd asked the people I worked with for help, I wish I'd focused less on losing weight, I wish I'd focused more on getting support around me. But I did what I thought was best at the time. Looking back can help us hold space for the parts of us that long for a different experience now. You can't go back, but you can be there for yourself in a different way now.

Because I was so thankful that we were at home after twelve days in the NICU, I felt terrified of mentioning how I was suffering emotionally and mentally. I thought, *You're lucky that your daughter is alive, how dare you be having a hard time right now?* I thought that I wasn't showing my very real gratitude if I tuned in to those tough feelings. So I ignored them for years, pushing them down without acknowledging anything.

If you're already a parent and you didn't have a traumatic birth like I experienced, or a birth experience at all because you adopted or became a parent in another way, there's still often this mix of pressure, gratitude, elation, and exhaustion all wrapped up in one. Anxiety, moments of depression, worrying, feeling overwhelmed, and other emotions may be ones that you've experienced as well. Even with an uncomplicated birth, as I had with my second child, I felt this sense of unbelievable gratitude but still noticed grief. When you commit to parenthood, you sign up for an unequal exchange with the little people that come into your life. This unequal exchange is healthy and necessary for children to be supported, but it's often taxing on the parents and it can feel like a loss of time, a loss of sense of self, and even a loss of identity. And when we experience loss, we're invited to grieve.

With the birth of my youngest daughter, I remember celebrating her arrival and being so thankful to have had an easeful experience and that she was healthy! I was allowed to leave the hospital twenty-four hours after giving birth and I just kept saying how grateful I was to be going home with my baby in this way this time. But I was also grieving how I'd no longer have all my attention for my oldest and what that would look like for both of us. I was grieving the shift this would have on my marriage, I was grieving the strength of my former body—there are so many things that we don't often get to talk about because we're scared of what people will think. Things that we're often shamed for mentioning. There's this belief that we're supposed to just focus on the elation, on the new baby, and that doesn't leave room for parents to be honest about what is happening internally without being ashamed for feeling what is normal. And when I think about this, I also feel a strong sense of empathy for all parents who struggle to parent.

I eventually talked about my feelings to a therapist, and I'll never forget the immense sense of validation I felt after sharing. I was so afraid of being judged. I was so afraid of getting odd looks, as I had received a few times when trying to share in the past. What I didn't realize was that I was attempting to share how I felt with people who didn't have the ability to understand me. They weren't able to hold space or show empathy for what I had gone through; maybe it was too deep, maybe they never allowed themselves to experience their own feelings in this way, or maybe they couldn't relate. Whatever the reason, I learned that their response to me was not evidence of me being wrong, but evidence that I was talking to the wrong person.

Parenting can and often does change who we are, what we allow in our lives, what we want for ourselves, and the way we relate to the world. It's a transformational change that takes a lot of emotional and mental space. Our sugar jars completely shift just at the thought of deciding we might want children. We begin to think about what we can keep, what we want to release, and perhaps if we need to expand our jars so that we can hold more energy. It serves us to acknowledge how we're feeling, even if it isn't talked about. It serves us to not be silent when we're uncomfortable or struggling. It serves us to be honest with ourselves so we can learn what we need. And it serves our children when we commit to being honest with ourselves. However good we think we are at hiding our struggles from them, they see them, so being honest with ourselves helps us be better parents for them, too. We won't ever be able to control every experience we'll have with our children, but we can learn to be there for ourselves as we're being there for them.

PARENTHOOD INVITES US TO HOLD BOTH AND . . .

Taking the time to be honest about how parenting is affecting you can help you cope with your emotions, create change if and where it's needed, and connect with others who may be struggling in similar ways. Finding parenting to be tough doesn't make you a bad person or parent, it makes you honest and human. And, yes, perhaps there are people who genuinely feel that they don't struggle with parenting and find it to be their absolute calling. That is wonderful and they should celebrate finding something that resonates deeply with them. But too often, there's an impression that we're supposed to feel specific emotions about things that haven't taken place. We are learning as we go.

Women especially are often painted as people who aren't fulfilled or living their full "destiny" or "potential" unless they're parents. And if a woman has decided to become a parent, there's this idea that they should be completely fulfilled by parenting and unfazed by the immense changes they've experienced. All people who become parents often experience a vast array of emotions, and they shouldn't be boxed into being made to feel or portray a particular kind of societal character based on what they're expected to be. We're also allowed to say no to parenting altogether. We're allowed to hold both the hard and joyful emotions.

So how can two or more things be true at the same time? Here are some examples:

- Parenting is a blessing and it's also incredibly energetically taxing.

- Parenting brings me joy and I also struggle with not having alone time.

- Parenting feels like a wonderful gift and it's also hard to not feel alone in it sometimes.

Take this time to think about three things that come to mind for you about parenting. Remember, if you're not a parent yet or you know you don't want to be a parent, you can still share your thoughts about what your experience was like being parented or about your decisions around parenting and how it's impacted you. Here are some examples from people who aren't parents yet or know they don't want to be parents:

- I enjoy spending time with children and I know parenting isn't something I'm interested in for me.

- There's nothing wrong with not wanting to have children and it's tough always feeling like I must explain myself to people who don't understand why I'd choose this.

- I'm excited to be a parent in the future and I worry about how parenting may change me.

- I can't wait to be a parent and I also feel like I don't know what to expect, and that's scary.

Giving yourself the freedom to explore holding more than one emotion empowers you to not have to fall into one category or the other. You're allowed to feel many things at once and it's okay if they're not always positive. Toxic positivity in parenting fools people into believing that no one *should be* struggling and that's just not the case. You can love your children and have a hard time with certain aspects of parenthood. You can love children and decide you don't want to be a parent. You can want children and decide that you want them at whatever age feels comfortable to you. Holding your multitude of emotions gives you the freedom to have what you actually want without feeling the pressure to conform.

REPARENTING YOURSELF

The topics of parenting and children often invite us to reflect on the way we were parented and what our childhood was like. Whether we desire to be parents or not, many of us are still healing childhood wounds in adulthood. Becoming a parent adds another layer to healing that we don't often see coming.

Most of the people I've worked with feel a deep desire to heal so that they don't pass on generational traumas and unhealthy lineage cycles to their children. The pressure sometimes translates to feeling like they're on a time crunch to heal so that their children, present or future, won't experience what they've experienced. It's tough to realize this, but the truth is that we can't stop our children from having negative experiences in life. We can prevent ourselves from continuing unhealthy cycles with our children that may have been played out with us. We can encourage healthy communication that hopefully ensures our children will feel comfortable coming to us when tough things occur. But we can't prevent them from experiencing the tough parts of life.

Understanding that our children will have tough times, just like we did, is hard, but it's also true. Accepting this helps us to detach from the idea that we'll always have control over what our children experience as they grow up. We can instill all the wisdom we own into them, and still they'll have the power of choice to live life on their own terms. As parents, we can do the best we can to provide a safe and loving environment for them where hopefully they'll feel empowered to grow into being exactly who they want to be, with our support along the way.

As we permit ourselves to redefine parenting of our children, it also gives us the opportunity to explore what reparenting ourselves would look like. What would it feel like to let ourselves off the hook from having to be the "perfect parent"? What would it feel like to be able to parent and have space for a life outside of caring for our children? What would it feel like to hold space for all of our emotions in the same way that we hold space for our children? What would it feel like to be kind, open, and unassuming about our children's exploration of themselves?

Now, let's flip these questions. Ask yourself: What would it feel like to provide that same kind of open curiosity for myself? What would it feel like to let myself off the hook from being and knowing all things? What would it feel like to hold space for all my emotions?

We don't have to be a parent to begin exploring how reparenting ourselves brings healing and understanding. So often we might see cycles that we had as children with our parental figures show up in our romantic relationships, our friendships, or even in our careers. At one workshop, a person shared in a break-off session, "I'm afraid that my trust issues with my parents are keeping me from getting close to other people. I want to trust them, but I don't know why . . . I don't believe them when they say they won't hurt me or disappoint me." Another person in the group shared, "I completely agree. Why would I give someone the opportunity to hurt me when I could keep them at arm's length?" There was a collective head nod of agreement that everyone shared.

I asked, "What would it feel like to know that the grown-up version of you has the power to protect not only the you that you are in this moment but all of the child and adult versions of you that have ever been hurt? When we have tough formative experiences, the person we were at that age sometimes decides to 'stick around,' usually unconsciously, to ensure that we don't encounter any circumstance or person that could expose us to those same painful emotions that we experienced when we were unable to fully protect or advocate for ourselves. We can understand why those hurt and scared versions of us would want to protect us. But it isn't the job of those younger versions of ourselves to protect us now because when we allow that child version of us to show up, we react with only the limited tools we had at the age, not the full breadth of tools we have as our full adult selves. Let that child part of you rest, it's tough, but let them rest. Then ask yourself: What do I need to feel safe? How do my relationships make me feel safe? Are there any situations or experiences that cause me to not feel safe? What support systems do I now have, through therapy or coaching, that can serve as a safe place to figure out tough experiences *should* they come up?"

I turned my head from side to side so that I could look at

every person in the group. Some were emotional, sharing, "I've never even thought about letting the child version of me rest." I replied, "Think about what a child would need. Rest, warmth, safety, empathy, security, love, and joy to name a few. Showing up for ourselves as adults means we get to offer ourselves the things we might've missed out on as children. It's a practice, but it helps to build self-trust, which can eventually allow us to learn how to extend trust to others."

Reparenting ourselves invites us to gently set boundaries and release barriers, which creates more openness so that we can learn to experience love without judgment or expectations.

CARING FOR YOUR SUGAR JAR

So many of us have situations where we are a caretaker for someone. And if not, we are the caretakers for ourselves. We may be a parent, we may take care of our parents, we may be a pet owner, perhaps we're a mentor, or maybe we dedicate our time to charitable organizations we care about. These energy exchanges are particularly special for our jars because we give and receive in very different ways. The reciprocity exchange is different. While we may be giving tangible things that in our society can very easily be translated into a monetary cost, like time, actual money, coaching, or attention, we may be receiving or filling our jars up with the positive feelings we get from being able to support the people or commitments we care about. Our love for them, our caring for them, and the knowing that they're okay because we're there fills us up. This is different than any other exchange where we may want tangible things back from the people we're in a relationship with or we want to know we'll be able to rely on them in return, e.g., in a romantic relationship or a friendship. But in these instances, our jars adjust to receiving in the way they can give, even if it's just a smile or a hug.

This is important because it reminds us that keeping our jars full isn't always about equal exchanges. Our jars can be filled easefully if we're doing it from a place of love and intent awareness about why we're giving without receiving in the traditional way. Our jars can be filled even if we're giving a lot if we're able to check in with ourselves regularly to assess when we need to take time to take care of ourselves. When we're entrusted with taking care of others, it becomes even more important that we prioritize our needs. With parenting, for example, from day to day you won't get to decide how much love, care, or attention your child will need. Your child wakes up and proceeds to ask for something (or throw a tantrum), signaling that they need you to show up even more for them than they would need on an easier day. Ensuring that we prioritize taking care of ourselves means that we'll have more flexibility when things go awry, as they will.

In relationships where you're the primary caretaker, they have complete and full access to your kitchen and your jar. They may come in and take one tablespoon of sugar or they may come in and take two cups. This is why it's important to manage the other relationships you're in with care and clarity because you'll want to make sure your jar is full enough for the primary responsibilities you have in your life.

WHAT ATTENDING TO YOUR JAR AS A PARENT OR CARETAKER MAY LOOK LIKE

- Waking up early before your children get up so you can have some quiet alone time.

- Relying on the community around you and taking support when it is offered.

- Allowing other relatives or family friends to help support with adult caretaking responsibilities.

- Being honest with yourself about what you can handle and how what you'd like to do maybe isn't a priority.

- Asking yourself what responsibilities or commitments may need to take a back seat so that you have enough time and attention for everyone (including you).

WHAT ATTENDING TO YOUR JAR WHILE REPARENTING YOURSELF MIGHT LOOK LIKE

- Finding safe spaces to share your feelings.

- Setting aside time to care for yourself in ways that make you feel seen and special.

- Giving yourself permission to play.

- Letting go of familial rituals that no longer resonate.

Next, think about things that you've experienced when you were parented that may be impacting the way you show up as a parent or in other relationships.

ASK YOURSELF:

- Do I want everything to be perfect because I'm afraid I'll "mess my kids up"?

- Do I not take time for myself because I'm afraid of how other people will judge me?

- Do I think taking care of others means sacrificing all of my time and attention for my kids?

- Am I afraid to set boundaries with my kids? Why?

- Am I afraid to set boundaries with my parents? Why?

- Am I afraid to do things differently than my family does them? How is this impacting my well-being? What would it be like to do what feels good to me, regardless of whether it resonates with others?

- Am I still angry about what I experienced in my childhood? What steps do I need to take to begin to process this now?

Now, let's look at your jar:

- How much of your energy is spent doing things because that was the way you were parented but those things don't actually resonate with you anymore?

- How much of your energy is spent doing things as a parent because boundaries aren't in place with your kids or partner?

- How much of your energy is spent doing things as a caretaker for family members that you could get help with?

- How much of your energy is spent doing things for other family members who can completely take care of themselves because that's how it's always been done?

ASK YOURSELF:

- What would it feel like to do what I want to do regardless of what others think I should be doing?

- What would it feel like to ask for help with some of my tasks sometimes?

- What would it feel like to put something that I always need (like toilet paper) on a subscription so it doesn't have to be on my to-do list?

- What would it feel like to have my children perform age-appropriate tasks that help them learn independence and I have some free time to do other things?

- How would it feel to set a boundary to stop answering inappropriate questions about why I choose not to parent or why I'm not parenting yet?

The intention is that you're constantly checking in with your jar to see if there are any cracks, if there are any leaks, if you notice whether the counter your jar is on is getting a bit messy, or if your jar seems less full. These things directly correlate to feeling overwhelmed, trying to keep everything together by yourself, needing better boundaries, caring for yourself when things are hard, and sometimes learning how to let things go.

My birth experiences left my jar with several cracks and leaks, sugar dispersed all over the kitchen, and I had no clear idea of how I was going to repair my jar or fill it again. I didn't even realize that my jar was in such need of care, because I was busy keeping up with everything else in my kitchen. Sometimes we are completely unaware of how detached we are from ourselves, especially when our time is dedicated to caring for others who need us. Your sugar jar serves as a reminder that you are in need of you, too.

Parenting also gives you another jar to manage. As a parent, you're not only responsible for your jar, you're now responsible for managing the jars of your children, which reside in your kitchen. Parenting or being a caretaker is the only time others' jars will reside in your kitchen. As your children grow up, they'll give signs that they're interested in having more responsibility for taking care of their jars or perhaps you'll assign them tasks for taking care of their jars. But overall, the responsibility of their jars is yours until the jar exchange is made and they begin building their own kitchens in their adult lives. Because you have full access and visibility to their jars, you're most likely filling them up in any way that you can in anticipation of what they'll need beforehand. Which is great; as parents we should provide for our children in all the ways we can. But knowing that you have your jar plus the jars of any children or people you're in charge of caretaking is more of a reason to be honest with yourself about what you'll need to be able to manage. To find balance, we have to be willing to admit what we need to give ourselves first.

ASK YOURSELF:

- Do I believe in balance?

- What does/would balance look like to me?

- What makes it hard to find balance daily?

- What's one thing that could help me feel more at ease?

- What's one thing, if possible, that I could do to free myself from doing that could give me more time for me?

As a parent, it's important to remember that just because the children we have are tiny, it doesn't mean their jars will be small. Some will need a lot of sugar to be taken care of, and again we never know what we're getting until we get them. We can love them and acknowledge that we may need to restructure our kitchen, our sugar-filling schedule, or we may need to limit the access others have to us while we adjust.

As we reparent ourselves, we may find that we're invited to get to know ourselves in a new way. Sometimes there's grief or regret for what we didn't receive as children. Sometimes there's an appreciation for the moments of support we did receive. We're caring for our sugar jars when we recognize how we can show up for ourselves now.

ASK YOURSELF:

- What would it feel like to be free of all of the self-imposed expectations I've set for myself that aren't working?

- How can I begin to let them go now?

- How would I talk to myself if those self-imposed expectations no longer existed?

Say It with Me

I can create, receive, and give all that I never experienced or saw growing up.

I give myself permission to be a student of parenting, which means I'm allowed to always be learning.

I am always a priority in my life.

9

THE STRONG ONES

It was 2011 and I was living in Valdosta, a small city in southern Georgia, practically touching the Florida border line. As a New Yorker, living in the South was such a new experience. I remember little things like being able to parallel park better than I could pull into a spot, as parallel parking was way more commonplace where I was from. Small moments like that often reminded me how far I was from what I considered to be home. Even though I'd been living in Valdosta for a few years at that point, I was in a constant adjustment phase as so much was changing in such a short amount of time. This was my first and only duty station while on active duty in the US Air Force.

My daughter's father deployed at the beginning of that year, when she was just four months old. Within six months of her birth, I'd gone from a traumatic delivery to being a twenty-four-year-old solo mom in the military trying to figure it all out. I was breaking. I didn't have an awareness of it yet, but each day was getting a bit tougher to get through. My daughter was an absolute angel of a baby, thank God, and was ALWAYS cheerful and easygoing and slept through the night every single night. Everyone mentioned how lucky I was that she was "such a good baby," and I knew it was a blessing *and* I was **still** struggling to keep up. I remember that I kept wondering when it was going to feel easier for me.

I felt overwhelmed, having just gone through one of the most traumatic moments of my life with my daughter's delivery, then being alone and going back to work when she was six weeks old as if nothing had ever happened. Not many people knew what had happened during my delivery, so I didn't feel comfortable sharing my feelings. And the military wasn't really a place for emotion; in fact, it was the place where I perfected shutting down my emotions completely. I'd already learned some of that as I was growing up, but I had it down to a science by then. In addition, I probably wouldn't have shared my emotions anyway because I didn't have any awareness that I had emotions about it. I was unaware that my current situation, raising a new baby while trying to get my very fatigued body and mind back in military shape, was contributing to overwhelming stress. I was literally just going through the motions.

In my mind at the time, this was just something that you pushed through. And I believed without a doubt that I was strong enough to withstand all of it. So I pushed myself, hoping that my keen sense of detail would help me out as I believed it always had. Without any consistent support around, a work schedule that was increasingly unpredictable and heavy, and no real structure, I just kept going.

Back then, sharing my emotions fell into one of two categories: sharing my excitement or sharing my anger. I had no idea that a multitude of feelings existed within a spectrum of intensity and that I could perhaps be feeling many of them at any given time. I was completely out of touch with the fact that I felt sad, scared, and disappointed. Instead I believed my lack of emotion was evidence of my resilience and strength. Not my detachment from myself.

As time went on, I started to feel anger at the people around me and wondered how they couldn't see that I was drowning. The lack of inquiry or concern from others added to my distress and eventually became more of a focus point for me than my actual well-being. I ended up in a discussion with a friend where I shared my lack of understanding at how no one had come to visit me or offer to help me since they knew I was doing everything alone.

The response was always the same. "You're handling yourself well, you're so strong" or "Not everyone is as strong as you, I couldn't imagine." I had a chat with a different friend about it, and they shared something with me that I will never forget. They said, "Yas, you always behave as if you have it together, so people don't think you need help. Maybe if you didn't seem so strong, people could be there for you." I thought to myself, *I'm f**king drowning. I have to scream for rescue while trying to keep myself afloat?* I later realized that perhaps they didn't have the ability to see me drowning because they were in the same body of water with me, barely holding on as well.

But still, I was pissed. So wait, I need to be "weak" in order to get help? I need to "fall flat on my face" in order to be seen? I need to "struggle" in order to show people that I needed them? Looking back, it's so interesting to see the aversion I had to those words because at that very moment in time I had *fallen flat on my face*, I was *struggling*, and my capacity to handle what I was going through was increasingly *weakening*. Within months from this discussion with my friend I had my first panic attack. I knew then that I really needed help, but there were two things happening: 1) I wanted to be strong and able to handle everything without anyone because I didn't want to be disappointed by people not showing up, plus it made me feel like I was accomplished by handling everything, and 2) I wanted people to show up for me without it meaning I was weak.

I had never felt so alone, but sharing what I needed felt impossible. I had never seen anyone receive help or assistance in a way that didn't come back to bite them. I was terrified of someone having "something over me" because I didn't often see help exchanged in a healthy and loving way.

I also felt that I was already asking for help, and that didn't seem to do anything but cause more conflict and distress. Those moments when I finally got the guts to reach out to someone and ask for help and received a bombardment of reasons that they couldn't show up would crush me.

And after all, there was still this part of me that believed that being strong was the very thing that got me to where I was. It was why I was so successful, so motivated, and able to handle all the things that were thrown my way. I was absolutely unwilling to be seen as anything but strong, as I believed it ensured that I was never going to be taken advantage of. I was in this tough space of desiring help and reciprocity but fearing what that meant about me. And because of that, the barriers I placed around myself had to be practically torn down piece by piece until I was finally willing to allow myself to be seen, by others and, most important, by myself.

Over time, strength began to feel like a burden. Because of my ability to push through, I was often left to deal with my stuff alone. But I also didn't realize how my identity as "strong" had taken on a new definition that allowed me to easily connect with doing it all myself because "no one would help me anyway," or so I thought. It was true that there were people in my life who weren't willing or able to show up the way that I needed them to, but it wasn't true that it would always be that way. It wasn't true that it could never change.

STRONG DOESN'T MEAN INVINCIBLE

It's tough work learning to redefine what strength looks like while making space for vulnerability. My skewed perception of strength meant that being seen as vulnerable was not an option as I thought it made me more at risk for harm. I was strong and so I believed that meant that I couldn't also receive support. I thought I needed to be completely burned out, overburdened, or stressed to ask or receive help. There was so much unlearning to do.

Anytime I need help from others, I'm invited to revisit what strength means to me. The big disconnect for a lot of strong folks is that they're able to endure trials and traumas while being detached from their emotions, so they believe they don't need the same assistance or support as anyone else. And this can create a barrier where we don't allow others to help us. Other times, self-proclaimed strong folks can feel angry about the reaction they receive when they finally ask for help, especially if it turns out negatively. The feeling might sound like "Why do we have to argue about how I didn't ask for help before, I'm asking now" or "Why do I have to appear helpless for you to show up?" or "Why do I always have to do it alone?"

It's also important to mention that when I was in my early twenties much of my beliefs about what I "should" be able to handle were based on what I'd seen and what I was witnessing at the time. I thought, *I'm not the first single mother, and I also won't be the last!* Or *I'm not the only person with a partner who was deployed,*

I just have to keep going. Instead of allowing my emotions to come forward, I stunted them.

Comparing what I was going through with what others were experiencing kept me from being kind to myself. Comparing myself with others was also unrealistic because I didn't realize that I didn't *really* know what anyone else was going through. I was comparing myself to what they were portraying, and based on the way I was portraying myself, it became clear that I had no real idea about how they were managing.

Over time I've learned that the strong ones are all of us. We might think there are those who get all of the support they desire, but we <u>all</u> have moments where we've felt burdened or overwhelmed, and instead of making space for that we just go through what we were experiencing without any space for softness, ease, or compassion. And when we are prone to toughness, it becomes a cycle that we continue over and over again, where it becomes increasingly hard to recognize our pattern.

We might tell ourselves that our strength not only allows us to power through our own issues, but in addition it gives us the power to support anyone and everyone else through their issues. We also become the one everyone else can rely on. And therefore many of us can only see outside ourselves, noticing what is happening around us and where we might be needed or what we aren't receiving rather than focusing on how we can give to ourselves within.

It's also tough to realize that being strong no matter what might be your defense mechanism to dealing with people who aren't interested in showing up for you. This may be true in some of your relationships with friends, family, or even parental figures. These relationships may have taught you that it isn't safe to need people.

SELF-PROCLAIMED STRONG ONES

Some of you chose strength as your form of armor because growing up you witnessed what could happen if for some reason the people around you didn't see you as strong. You may have seen those you love be taken advantage of, and so strong felt like safety.

Or perhaps you identify as strong because it feels good to feel reliable and secure, which are actual attributes of strength. But those attributes don't mean that you don't want reciprocity from others. And sometimes, when we experience disappointment after letdown after frustration, we decide that we're not going to sign up for that anymore. That being strong means we'll get through, no matter what, with or without anyone else.

"BUT THEY NEED ME" OR "I DO IT BETTER"

Many of you have been conditioned to believe that when a partner, friend, or even your career states that they "need" you, all your needs no longer matter as much or they should go right out of the window. But let's unpack the word "need." Why do they need you? What are you giving them that no one else (including them-selves) can? How can you begin to decide whether this need is based on love, manipulation, or perhaps your desire to be around people that **you need to need you** so that you feel desired?

Sometimes we carry an unconscious pride and confidence in our ability to do things "better" than others because sometimes . . . it's true. But that doesn't mean that you should be the absolute choice every single time. It often becomes one of the toughest parts of unlearning the "always strong" persona because always doing it better often equates to receiving external validation, which can feel good.

What we may not realize is how exhausted, overwhelmed, and stressed we also feel by not only being the one who's called on to "do it right," but the pressure we put on ourselves to live up to the idea that we're the ones whom everyone can always count on. There's nothing wrong with being dependable; in fact, this is a wonderful trait. But it's absolutely impossible to always get it right or to always be available when called on. Dependability is not the same as perfection. Consistency is not the same as perfection.

ASK YOURSELF:

- Does someone's need of me help me feel stronger, validated, or necessary?

- How can I be strong and worthy of connection without fully supporting everyone else's weight?

- How might I be self-sabotaging myself by believing the story that without me the particular "thing" that they "need" won't happen? How can I rewrite that story?

P.S. You don't need to have a conversation with anyone to rewrite that story, you can say yes to a new story right now.

TYPES OF STRONG ONES

Sometimes we don't realize that we're behaving as a strong one because we believe that it's an inherent part of who we are. Many strong ones can't even remember a time when they would've been able to equally rely on others. Other strong ones may remember the exact incident that changed who they were going forward. Wherever you fall on this spectrum, recognizing some of the ways that you perform tasks or show up as the strong person can help you to be more aware of what may need to shift within.

THE RESPONSIBLE CHILDREN

A lot of the people I work with, including myself, are the oldest child in their family and identify with feeling that they've had more responsibility or pressure than their siblings. Of course, there are so many sides to the story, right? And it's also true that there are younger siblings who've had to carry more than what belonged to them. What's important is to focus on how you're feeling rather than trying to convince others that your feelings are valid. It doesn't need to be valid in their eyes for it to be real to you. And if you identify as an oldest child or a child who has had to carry more responsibility than most children normally do, much of your programming may be wired around you being able to predict what may be needed before it's asked of you. Much of your identity may also be tied into being the strong, reliable, "I can handle anything" responsible one.

For me, having this belief definitely affected the way I approached those early days of motherhood. I thought I'd been "training my whole life" for this very moment of feeling overwhelmed. I didn't realize it was time to learn a different way of leaning into strength. Over time, your early adulting pours into your actual adult years and you continue the same role with everyone. Your friends, family, job, and perhaps even your partner see you as the one who's always there to pick up the ball even before it has a moment to drop. No matter what you have going on, no matter what's being asked of you in other places, you show up.

PERFECTIONISM

Many of us feel like we're the strong one in our relationships because somehow we always do things the "right" way. You may have found that when you've solicited help from others, if the task wasn't carried out with the same tenacity and vigor that you would've applied to it, then perhaps it feels half done or incomplete. In addition, when the strong one *finally* asks for assistance and it doesn't appear to have been carried out with the same intense enthusiasm that we would've applied, it feels like a hurtful joke. "I've finally asked for help, and this is the help I get? This is why I **never** ask."

But what's often in the way of the strong one's allowing in help from others is the tendency to believe the idea that help has to be provided in a particular way in order for it to be accomplished or "right." What if there wasn't any "right" way to do everything and by allowing others to help you accomplish a task, even if it's done differently than you would've done it, you receive the help you desire? What if their showing up and doing the best they can, for you, was what mattered? Releasing the idea that anything has to be done "right" in order for it to be done is powerful.

I've talked extensively about how my desire to "get it right" had burned me out in many ways. And it burns all of us out. When our desire is to never fail, we keep ourselves in a cycle of exhaustion that can't end until we're ready to make a change, and change can be tough. As a recovering perfectionist myself, this remains something I have to remind myself to let go of regularly. When dealing with perfectionism, we've often intertwined others' ability to perfectly meet our needs with their level of love or respect for us. "If they loved me, then they would do it the way I asked" or "If they cared about me, then they would make sure this was done right and I wouldn't have to redo it. I should've just done it myself."

You can intellectually understand that you're not perfect but also recognize that your perfectionism has helped you stand out, so it may feel scary to put the "shield of perfectionism" down.

Ask yourself: How can I learn to show up without what feels like such an important part of who I am? How can I learn that perfectionism is not what makes me valuable to others?

THE STRONG FRIEND

"I am not your strong friend. I am supportive and I'll show up for you. You can count on me to be consistent. But I won't be able to show up as you need me to without being held as well. I know sometimes it may look like I have it all figured out, but I don't. I worry and need help, too, even though I'm still learning how to talk about it. I am thankful you know you can rely on me. I am thankful for our relationship. I am thankful I've been able to hold all of the people who matter to me most. But I am surrendering that responsibility that was never mine. You still have me, just not all of me."

I wrote this in 2020 as an ode to the strong friends but also as an opportunity for people who identify as "the strong one" to make a promise to themselves. It's important to shift the narrative for yourself and remind yourself that it's okay to be there for yourself sometimes.

It's okay to be someone everyone relies on. But it's also okay that you have others you can rely on, too.

THE PROBLEM WITH
"YOU'RE SO STRONG"

People who are perceived to be emotionally stronger than others are often inundated with verbal confirmations of how strong they appear to be. Perhaps you shared with someone how you just went through a scary and unexpected experience, and the response may have sounded like "Wow, you're so brave, I couldn't imagine." Or maybe you went through a divorce or breakup and a friend or family member shares "You're so strong, you'll be fine." Anytime a tough thing comes up you hear some version of "You're the strongest person I know."

If you haven't been on the receiving end of this, you might be thinking, "What's wrong with telling someone how strong they are? Isn't that supportive? Doesn't it serve as a reminder of how they have the strength to get through this? Isn't it a testament to how they're able to get through things that I don't think I could get through if I was in their shoes? Is this not an affirmation?"

There's nothing wrong with letting someone know that you admire their strength and willingness to be brave. But it's a very different experience when that person doesn't have friends or family who are able to see the struggles, the fears, and the vulnerability and instead consistently witness their perceived strength, which they may not even feel they have or want. Because, remember, this tough experience, although it may be grooming them for growth, is something they most likely aren't thrilled to be going through. They want and deserve to be seen as human.

Here's a list of alternative things to say to someone instead of "You're so strong":

- This sounds really hard for you. How can I be there for you?

- Would you like me to listen or try to help you with this?

- How can I support you?

- Would you like to share more about what you're going through?

- I know this is a tough time, I'm so sorry and I'm here for you.

- I don't know what to say except that I'm here for you.

- I know there will be another side, but until then please know that I'm here for you.

- This is a tough part of your current journey, and I'll be by your side as you get through this.

Customize the above language to make it sound like you, but the important part is to center their experience and show support in the ways that you can.

If you've been on the receiving end of hearing "You're so strong" in response to the tough experiences that you've gone through, it may feel like you're being silenced. It can sound like "You're so strong so we don't need to talk about this or dedicate any time to what you're going through." I know that it may be tough to consistently hear when sometimes you just want someone to say "I'm so sorry you're going through this. How can I help?" It may also feel true that hearing about your strength in the past served as a source of validation and perhaps even empowered you, which makes the whole thing feel uneasy and confusing. Know that it's okay for your needs to differ based on the type of situation you're going through and for the support you need to change based on how you feel.

Here's a list of replies when someone says "You're so strong":

- Thanks, but I don't feel strong at the moment. Do you mind if I talk about how this is hard for me?

- I know in the past I've been able to move through something like this with what may have appeared as "ease," but this time it's a bit different. Can we talk about that?

- That's interesting that it looks that way because I'm actually really struggling right now.

- It's tough when you share that I'm strong when I'm trying to share how I don't feel so strong right now and actually need support. It isn't helping me in the way you might think.

[NOTE: Remember, in previous chapters we talked about understanding other people's ability to be there for us based on how they've shown up with us in the past. This particular prompt may not be fully understood by someone who has shown that they aren't able to support you emotionally and might be better for someone who is really trying to be there but perhaps doesn't understand how saying "You're so strong" or a variation of it might be hurting you.]

BEING STRONG IN ROMANTIC PARTNERSHIPS

In romantic partnerships, sometimes the strong ones feel like they can take on anything! Debt? I can handle it. Trust issues? Throw it my way, I've got it. Infidelity issues? Don't worry, I can fix it. The strong ones can often see red flags as a challenge that they've built up just the right amount of tolerance to handle instead of seeing that this particular partner may not be the best fit for them.

Of course everyone comes with their challenges and issues. However, just because you can take it doesn't mean you have to and that's sometimes hard to realize.

Romantic partnerships can also be a place where the strong ones tend to project a lot of their needs on their partners. You might feel like you're always strong for everyone else, and this is supposed to be the one place that you can completely be supported and held. But your partner may not have signed up to hold you while you're holding everyone in your world.

PUSHING YOURSELF OUT OF YOUR COMFORT ZONE VS. PUSHING THROUGH

Sometimes we confuse the strength of pushing ourselves out of our comfort zones with pushing through or suffering through. We usually need to push ourselves out of our comfort zones for success, achievement, or even for connection because sometimes even vulnerability requires some gentle nudging.

If we're working out, and we don't feel any pain, we might go a little harder even though it's uncomfortable because we want to reach a goal. If we're running a business, we might sign up for a speaking engagement that feels scary because it's new but will propel us to another level. Or we might tell a romantic partner or friend our true feelings even though it's scary to not know how they'll respond. This is often a healthy version of nudging ourselves to try something that has potential positive benefits.

Pushing through often requires us to ignore our emotions in order to do it. We may become unconscious to our fears, discomfort, and boundary violations, and instead suffer through. Pushing through often comes with dread, not excitement. Pushing through often comes with shame, not encouragement. Pushing through often comes with the energy of "I should do this," not "I get to do this."

Many people who have been placed in the strong category or identify as strong push through in the name of family, friends, culture, and sometimes validation.

WHEN WILL I FINALLY BE SEEN?

You might be thinking, "When will people see that I'm struggling? When will people see that I'm overwhelmed? When will people understand that my strength doesn't mean that I'm not human and that I have needs, too? When will they see my softness? When will I see my softness?"

It's important to mention that there is **nothing** wrong with being strong. **Our goal is to redefine strength so that your humanness is also visible.**

A STRONG JAR STILL NEEDS SUPPORT

If you are someone who identifies as a strong one, your jar is most likely often empty, although you may not realize it because you might tell yourself that it's full with all of the people and places you support. Your life may feel filled with things to do, but your energy is consistently drained. You've gotten so used to operating without any nourishment, replenishment, or assistance that empty begins to feel normal. In fact, having sugar in your jar may be a bit uncomfortable and you might sign yourself up for another thing to do as it feels like you have sugar to burn.

Being a strong person in the lives of the people you care about doesn't mean you don't also get to be a strong and reliable person for YOU. There is strength in learning to receive, too.

Your jar is glass, just like everyone else's. It is durable and able to withstand the elements. But under too much pressure, it can crack and even break. There are infinite ways to replenish your jar. But you also have to be willing to recognize what you need, put boundaries in place, and stop forcing yourself to continue behaving as if you're not susceptible to the same things everyone else goes through.

When you're filling your sugar jar after periods of neglect, your jar needs extra attention, support, and care from you and your community. Regularly filling your jar and putting the lid on it can undo so much of the "strong no matter what" cycle and forces you and others to recognize that even you are human! You can say no, you can step back, you can recharge, and you can direct that attention toward yourself.

Being constantly referred to as strong by others can be an escape sometimes for them to not have to be in a reciprocal relationship with you. Because of their beliefs about your perceived strength, they may not feel that you need someone to be there for you, that, in fact, you solely serve as a support for others.

The people in these relationships show up to your sugar jar with containers so that they can get every cup of sugar available. The moment you put a bit of sugar back in your jar, they're right back in your kitchen to take it for themselves. It's important to remember that some people know that this kind of relationship is possible with you and may be present and waiting at your jar for the opportunity to have access to your energy without ever having to give.

We referenced earlier how boundaries aren't the only thing you need to protect your jar. Yes, if you're lacking some boundaries it's important to put them in place, but it's also important to unpack the story you believe that says the strong one is who you are and therefore how you should show up in every area of your life. Believing that you are stronger than most and can handle more than most creates an atmosphere in your kitchen where people are regularly lined up to access your jar, and instead of you seeing your kitchen as a sacred place for you, you begin to think of your kitchen as a restaurant that you run. Where people come and place their orders and you supply them.

One of the things that I love about sugar as a reference for our energy is that when you hold one granule of sugar in your hand you're able to feel the roughness, size, and texture of that one granule. But if there's a cup of sugar and you put your hand in it, the sugar feels softer, and each granule loses itself in the other. It feels more delicate.

I find that this is also true about us. That our energy is much softer, delicate, and flows with more ease when we're able to hold all of it within ourselves, discerning carefully before we give it away. This isn't about not giving parts of us at all, as we will say yes to others sometimes. It's about not giving all of you away and ensuring that there's always some left for you to enjoy.

HOW CAN I FILL MY JAR?

GETTING SUPPORT FROM THE *RIGHT* PEOPLE

Not everyone will be able to show up for you and help you. This is a fact that also doesn't mean you have to do life alone. When you've been so afraid of allowing people in because you've mostly had yourself to rely on, it's tough getting used to people showing up. But when you cultivate relationships with people who want to show up or allow the people who've been asking to show up to be there for you, you begin to effectively break the cycle of solo life.

REDEFINING WHAT STRONG MEANS

When I realized that I needed community to thrive, I finally began accepting those offers for help. I'll be honest, it took me years to fully allow people in, but each step helped me redefine what strength meant to me.

You also get to define what strong means for you, and if the current definition you have doesn't make space for your humanness, softness, ease, joy, peace, and beyond, it may be time to create a new one.

Does your kitchen feel like a stopping point for people to get what they need whenever they need it? Do you often feel like your sugar is completely depleted?

What would your definition of strong look like if it allowed the support of others while giving you the freedom to be fully supportive of yourself?

THINK BEYOND BOUNDARIES

Boundaries will help you fix so many leaks within your jar as we talked about in a previous chapter, however, they won't help you fix everything because we can't set boundaries for things that we don't know are issues. So think beyond boundaries and build awareness around how you can prevent yourself from continuing to be only known as the strong one in relationships and to stop yourself from committing to the role in future commitments.

ASK YOURSELF:

- What's similar about these situations when they occur?

- Does the person say things that attract me to being in the strong role? (E.g., Just because someone says "You're so reliable" or "You handle tough situations so well" doesn't mean that you now have a license to always be that person. There will be times when you handle things with ease and there will be other times where you'll need more support. Both are okay.)

GIVE YOURSELF PERMISSION
TO BE STRONG AND . . .

Can't it be true that you're strong and soft? Strong and vulnerable? Strong and require support? Strong and in flow? Strong and have boundaries? Strong and gentle with yourself? Strong and capable of receiving help? Strong and open to reciprocity?

When holding both your strength and your humanness, remember that it's okay to need help. It's okay to not carry every-

thing for everyone. It's okay to not always be the person who
fixes everything for everyone. It's okay to "crack under pressure"
and require support and/or assistance. It's normal to not have to
carry everything on your own, even though that may be what you
thought you'd always have to do.

Say It with Me

I am stronger when I let people be there for me.

I am stronger when I acknowledge my limits.

I am stronger when I resist being someone else's everything.

10

AM I HEALING?

I was waiting in line to pick my daughter up from preschool. She'd only been in school a few weeks, and there were so many new things to adjust to, particularly the process during pickup and drop-off. The school had a system for checking your child in and out that was very particular, and if you didn't get it exactly right, it wouldn't register your child as signed in or out. If for some reason you didn't follow the instructions exactly or perhaps just forgot to sign your child in or out it cost you a two-dollar fee each time. Even though this required tedious attention to detail, it didn't upset me or cause any emotional reaction from me, so I just did my best to follow the instructions.

While waiting for my little one to get her shoes out of her cubby, another parent walked up and said to me, "Isn't this sign-out process

the worst? Who has time to remember all these steps? How dare
they charge a fee for something like this? It makes me sick." I could
understand their frustration. We already had a lot to do to get these
little ones ready to leave the house and dropped off, so having to
worry about the possibility of a fee, which is small but could add up
quickly, is an additional step that most of us would rather not have.

But in that moment, while this parent was waiting for me to join
them on the "I can't stand this either" bandwagon, I did a check-in
with myself. I reminded myself that the sign-out process wasn't both-
ering me. This helped me to remember that I didn't have to join
this parent in the experience they were individually having. I could
listen to them or just be there without saying yes to the invitation to
drain my energy. And since I really couldn't find anything to say that
could be helpful and that felt true to me, I decided that I didn't have
to say anything. Instead, I chose to listen and gave them a smile that
said "I hear you" when they were finished. They smiled back.

While driving back home, I thought about how that small interaction was such a big sign of my ability to be grounded in my experience without taking on anyone else's emotions, without feeling
responsible to *do* anything, and without feeling the need to perform
in any way. I held my boundaries without being harmful. In the past,
an invitation like that would've manifested in me joining someone
else's negative energy. And no matter how valid their experience is
for them, I don't have to merge with them. I can keep the lid on my
jar and keep my kitchen door closed. I realized that this was what
healing looked and felt like in real time.

Before I was able to walk myself through experiences like these and recognize my growth, I often wondered when I'd be able to know that healing was happening in my life. Was all the work I was putting in worth it? Would things always feel this hard? And what would life look like when healing had taken place?

Now that you're toward the end of this book, you might be thinking, "Okay, so what now? I've implemented all the things, I've put all the boundaries in place, and I really need to know, is any of this working?" If you answered, "No, I'm not fully healed," you're correct! If you answered, "Yes, I believe I'm healed," you're also correct, BUT with the caveat that there will be more healing to come. Why? First, I don't get to tell you if you're doing "healing" right, you decide whether it feels right, so if you think you're healed in a particular area of your life, at this very moment, you are because you said you are. You're in charge of discerning whether your healing is improving your life, and this is a good thing because if healing was measured based on other people's beliefs or experiences, it would never fit what you need. But also if you're a living person who is connected to people, places, or things, there will be situations that come up that will require you to:

- Investigate behaviors or emotions that are coming up within you.

- Investigate potential triggers coming up within you.

- Investigate behaviors or emotions that are being projected toward you.

- Set boundaries with or without tough conversations.

- Talk about emotions or behaviors with others.

- All of the above.

In almost every other area of our lives, when we commit to something, we get external feedback on how we're doing. If you're a parent, your feedback comes from your children. If you're in a partnership, your feedback comes from your partner. If you run a business, your feedback comes from your customers. And in all those situations the thoughts, ideas, and feelings you have are **also** valid. But in healing work, we're invited to lean on our own feedback more than anyone else's.

When I did that check-in with myself before deciding how I would respond to that parent, I took a very quick trip to my kitchen and assessed my sugar jar. It's also helpful to know that when you're a frequent visitor to your kitchen and sugar jar, your understanding of what will drain you or fill you gets more easeful. I already know that any sort of performing quickly drains my jar and that the effects of showing up in any way other than how I really feel have a lasting impact on the environment in my kitchen. When I choose others over myself, my kitchen and jar always suffer and there is always cleanup to do. Sometimes we want to believe that healing is an equation, and if you endure X amount of suffering, or X amount of learning, or X amount of lessons, you add on Y amount of healing and will finally get to the status of <u>healed</u>.

With that mind-set, healing becomes another thing that we add to our to-do list rather than something we look forward to. Healing becomes a chore rather than a nourishment. Healing becomes something we loathe rather than something we enjoy. And healing can also become something that we're constantly trying to make happen through force rather than something we're allowing to gently unfold in our lives. Healing can start to feel stressful and overwhelming if it becomes a consuming part of our lives rather than a support function that we can turn to when needed. The truth is, healing is taking place even in the smallest ways when we choose ourselves, like not engaging in a conversation that doesn't feel good. Every little action that we take matters and fills our jar.

When healing becomes something that we think of with a finish line attached, we might also begin to measure ourselves against others, believing that we've "graduated" or perhaps even excelled to a "graduate school or PhD" level of healing. But there are no healed and unhealed people. We've created this pedestal within wellness that makes people whom we've deemed unhealed to not be on the same level as those who are healed, which is untrue because we are ALL still healing.

Healing takes place in the everyday small ways we say yes to ourselves. I remember not knowing how to say no to conversations where others were gossiping. There were so many times that I knew I was saying yes, even if it was a passive yes, to something that I **knew** was draining my jar. The more I ignored my discomfort, the easier it was to keep ignoring it. But the more I showed up for myself, the easier it was to remember that it was possible.

You might be thinking, "That was such a small interaction with that parent. How could it truly hold any power?" The truth is, we learn so much from doing the small things. Before that interaction, I knew that it was okay not to have the *right* thing to say, <u>but</u> I still didn't know how that would play out in real life. What would it feel like to have someone ask me to show up for them in a way that I knew wasn't my role? It's through action that we recognize we can survive the awkward moments, we can survive the uncomfortable parts of holding our ground and setting boundaries, and we can survive not being the savior.

I also completely understand why you'd want to be done with healing. This work is **tough**. It requires a lot of time and attention and sometimes when we decide to choose ourselves, we lose people and things we never wanted to live without. We recognize new attributes in people that we didn't know were contributing to our stress. We learn new information about ourselves that we weren't consciously aware of. Sometimes we learn that a complete overhaul of our lives and relationships is the only way forward, and that's scary work. It can feel like the stakes for choosing our healing journey are incredibly high.

We commit to healing so that we can live a life that's filled with blessings, abundance, joy, peace, freedom, and everything that feels true to you. We commit to healing, so that when all those beautiful blessings arrive, we know how to make space for them. We commit to healing so we can openly receive blessings and ask for help when we need it. And when the tough times, hard-to-figure-out decisions, projections from others, internal triggers, and boundary violations arrive, we're able to hold ourselves through the process of determining what we need, advocating for it, and still holding the enjoyable parts of life, too. Healing gives us access to our *real* lives because we're living for ourselves.

Ultimately, thank goodness we'll always have the option to access our healing whenever we want to. Imagine if we were stuck where we are right now? Even though we may be in a wonderful place and worlds away from where we were, we get to choose whether we stay in this spot, and that's the beauty of healing and growth. We can stand proudly in who we are in this very moment and marvel about all the amazing work we've done to get to where we are. It was brave work. It was challenging work. And yet we committed. We can hold both our celebration for who we've become while recognizing we're still on the journey.

Ask yourself these questions, and reflect on how, no matter how small, you've begun to change the way you show up for yourself. It can be in the last five years or in the last five minutes. And even if after you advocate for yourself you have a moment where you don't set a boundary or you people-please, remember to have grace for yourself. Remember to be kind to yourself. Remember that you're still a student to this forever educational journey.

- How do I make positive decisions for myself now that I wouldn't have made before?

- How does it feel to know that I can make it through tough times? That I can learn from past experiences that were hard?

- How does it feel to own more of my autonomy than I did before?

- How does it feel to recognize my power?

- How does it feel to know that I'm worthy of love and acceptance?

- How does it feel to stand in my truth, even if I have to stand in it alone?

- How does it feel to have the choice to choose something completely different than my ancestors or lineage chose before me?

- How does it feel to own the breaking of generational curses WITHOUT taking full responsibility for everyone's healing around me?

- How does it feel to say no without an explanation?

- How does it feel to check in with myself first before I decide to commit to anything?

- How does it feel to know that change is still possible, even in the places where I'm still working on healing?

As we continue to choose our healing journey, we continue to choose ourselves, the parts we enjoy and the parts we're learning to accept and love no matter what. Be willing to give yourself what you need by taking breaks when you need to, celebrating your ability to keep choosing you, and releasing the distraction that is trying to get to a finish line.

I HEAR YOU, BUT
AM I DOING IT RIGHT?

After you learn how to tap into a new healing tool, the natural thought is "Am I doing this right?" Healing is one of the few areas where it is genuinely hard for others to tell you if it's right, although professionals, coaches, and spiritual teachers can help you discern if "right" translates to the actual outcome you're seeking. Because that is what "right" means. Are you living as you said you wanted to?

For example, if you're dating and you meet someone who seems really nice, you might be thinking:

Okay I . . .

- Checked in with how I'm feeling.

- Put healthy boundaries in place.

- Used my intuition to discern if this feels like a match.

But then other thoughts might seep in like:

- But wait, was that my intuition telling me this feels great or was that my fear?

- Am I ignoring something? This seems so great.

- I want this to work and I'm nervous I'm not following my instincts because I'm trying to enjoy myself on this date.

Just because you've learned some tools, myself included, it doesn't mean you won't have fears, intrusive thoughts, or concerns about choosing the "right" things for yourself. Anxiety may still come up even when you're healing. Feeling overwhelmed may still come up even when you're healing. You may still make decisions that don't work out even when you're healing.

So the better questions than "Am I doing this right" are:

How do I feel? Am I comfortable? Does this feel safe? Do I feel safe? Do I feel supported? Am I ignoring any of my feelings?

You are doing it right if you're comfortable where you are. You are doing it right if the changes you're seeking are coming to fruition. And if there comes a time when it doesn't feel right, you're completely empowered to change it.

MAKE HEALING FIT <u>YOUR</u> LIFE

One of the most powerful things that we can do for ourselves is to take complete ownership over what we choose to believe and how we make those beliefs fit our lives. If someone else's definition of boundaries doesn't work for you, don't take it in as a part of your wisdom. Only allow in what works for you.

I'd like you to go through the topics in this book that really stood out to you. The ones that really helped you to feel supported, seen, heard, and/or understood. Or perhaps the ones that helped to define experiences that you weren't able to define for yourself before. Now, I'd like you to redefine those topics in a way that helps them become more than something you've read that resonates, but something that actually fits your life.

For example, if we're talking about boundaries, I defined them in this book as: Boundaries are the rules or structures that we put in place that manage the way we interact with the people, places, things, and commitments we have in our lives.

Your definition of boundaries for your life might look like: Boundaries help me regain power over my life. When I set boundaries, I'm saying yes to myself. When I have boundaries in place, I don't feel as overwhelmed as I used to. I feel like I can manage my life when I have boundaries.

When you redefine these topics, you're taking ownership of them and making them make even more sense to you. It doesn't matter what I or anyone else thinks about boundaries, for example, when you're going through a hard time in a relationship and you're trying to figure out how to make boundaries fit for you. What will matter then is what you feel, need, and think about boundaries, and subsequently how you can then act on your own behalf.

GROWTH VS. HEALING

Growth and healing aren't the same and don't always take place together. You can heal things without experiencing growth and thank goodness we can grow and attain movement without having healed something. We're not always conscious of what needs to be healed, and things that need healing reveal themselves sometimes because of our growth. For example, you might be experiencing growth in your business but you realize that you have a hard time accepting the praise from that growth, because there's a part of you that needs to be healed to let the admiration in.

Allow growth to take place without healing. Allow healing to take place without growth. Sometimes things will develop and reveal themselves without any clear understanding of why they're happening in the order that they are. Release yourself from the responsibility of making it all make sense and instead witness and experience the gift, knowing better and doing better, as Dr. Maya Angelou would say.

GRIEVING WHO WE WERE

As we continue on our healing journey, there can be several points where we begin to look back at who we used to be. Reminiscing can come with pain and it can also come with excitement. Sometimes we miss parts of who we used to be because we miss who that version of us was able to be connected to. We might also miss how things seemed "easier" even though they may have been harmful. We might even look back and still feel guilt because of what we've walked away from or resentment because of what we feel we've lost. Other times, we look back and are so thankful for how far we've come while still recognizing what we believe "could've been" if we were who we are today back then.

Even when we're growing and healing, grief is usually right alongside us as we remove things, shift things, change things, and overcome things. When we're working on gaining new beliefs or a new way of being, it often requires us to let go of something else, which can trigger grief. No matter how long we've been in the healing process, grief can still be tough to navigate. Remembering to make space for grief as you heal can help you handle all of the emotions that come forth.

It's okay to miss parts of who you were. It's okay to sometimes remember nostalgic moments where there was also pain. It's okay if sometimes you wish you could go back because this side of healing feels lonelier. And it's okay if you're trying to find your way with the large amount of time and availability you now have because you set boundaries and say no to people-pleasing. Even the positive changes sometimes come with grief and knowing that it's an emotional process that can remain with us helps us to realize that it's also a part of this healing journey. We don't have to work to try to figure out how to get rid of grief. We don't have to pretend grief doesn't exist just because we're making positive changes. Grief is often a part of healing.

HEALING WON'T AUTOMATICALLY KEEP YOU FROM . . .

- Doubting yourself sometimes.

- Saying the "wrong" things.

- Getting upset or angry (in fact, healing may allow you to finally understand where that emotion is coming from).

- Having anxiety, or fears, or concerns, or worries (although you may feel more equipped to support yourself through these feelings).

- Having arguments sometimes (although healing can help you learn to walk away from unnecessary conversations that are unhealthy or harmful).

- Struggling with worthiness.

- Feeling like you don't belong or struggling with building community.

- Having to cope with a loud and sometimes obnoxious inner critic.

- Facing fears around vulnerability.

I still feel a twinge of discomfort when I think about the time a friend shared with me, in our group of friends, that I was intimidating to them. I remember feeling so hurt as I'd finally thought I'd found a group of folks I could relate to. I still feel the discomfort that comes up when I think about my first sugar jar workshop at a venue and right before I went on my point of contact shared with me, "I am shocked this many people showed up, being who you are, I thought maybe twenty or less would show." Healing helps us become more in touch with our feelings, it doesn't mean that we won't still struggle. It doesn't mean that we won't encounter tough times.

But healing does help us understand our choices. When we have our healing voice inside of us, it can help us ask ourselves questions that can guide us toward our true feelings.

Doubting yourself sometimes:

But what if you're exactly where you're supposed to be? What about all the work you did to get here?

Saying the "wrong" things:

What would it feel like to apologize?

Getting upset or angry (in fact, healing may allow you to finally understand where the emotion is coming from):

Why are you angry? What do you need in this moment?

Having anxiety, or fears, or concerns, or worries (although you may feel more equipped to support yourself through these feelings):

What is happening around you (in your life) when your anxiety, fears, concerns, or worries come up? What stories are you telling your-self? How can you get support in these moments?

Having arguments sometimes (although healing can help you learn to walk away from unnecessary conversations that are un-healthy or harmful):

Is there something you're afraid of that you need to share? Is there something you need?

Struggling with worthiness:

What is happening around you that is bringing up feelings of unwor-thiness? What would it feel like to take a moment to name all of the ways and reasons that you're already worthy?

Feeling like you don't belong or struggling with building com-munity:

What do you think it will mean if you belong with these particular people or in this particular group? Whom do you already belong to (including yourself)?

Having to cope with a loud and sometimes obnoxious inner critic:

What would it feel like to fact-check your inner critic (see chapter 4)? What would it feel like to share with someone you love or trust what you're struggling with internally?

Facing fears around vulnerability:

In the times in the past when you have been vulnerable, what positive experiences did you have, if any? What negative experiences did you have, if any? What would it feel like to choose vulnerability for you, without any expectations?

TAKING CARE OF YOUR
SUGAR JAR AND KITCHEN

As exciting as kitchen renovations can be, there is often some stress involved because it can take a lot of time, money, and energy, aka sugar, to get them accomplished. Sometimes we start a renovation purely out of choice and desire. We have the resources to dedicate to the project and so we create a plan to bring our vision to life. Other times, there's maintenance that's been needed for quite some time that we ignored because we didn't have the time or resources to dedicate our attention to it. When we ignore the maintenance, we put ourselves in a position where the repairs to our kitchen might go from "something we get to do" to a more urgent matter and it becomes "something we have to do now." As we all walk along our healing journey, we'll have moments where we find ourselves planning our kitchen reno and enjoying the process of being able to tend to ourselves, our atmospheres, our money, and our relationships with grounded attention. And we'll also have moments where there's been damage, or a pipe has burst, or a window is cracked and now we're rushing around trying to find the best tools, time, and wisdom to help us urgently fix the problem.

The wonderful thing about healing is that we always have the opportunity to change something if it no longer works. If we went with the premise that "we're healed," then things are fixed and stuck as they are. No matter what we learn going forward, we wouldn't feel like we have the right to update it because we've already fixed the "problem." *"Healed" closes the door. "Healing" ensures that we can update whenever we need to.*

In addition to kitchen renovations, we've talked extensively about the kinds of repairs we might need to make to our jars to provide a safe and secure place for our sugar to reside. But in addition to repairs, we may also decide to increase the size of our jars or decrease them for many different reasons. Perhaps you recognize that you'll need more sugar to provide for your family and so you increase your jar size. You have the option of bringing in a whole new glass jar or you can visualize using heat to expand the jar or decrease it. Whatever feels more comfortable for you. You might also realize that you've been spending more time keeping your jar full with sugar and you don't actually have a need for the amount of sugar that's in it. Maybe you just left your job or you downsized your responsibilities. Having the option to increase or decrease your jar size is important because you're the one who has to keep it full, no matter the size. Having more than you need or less than you need all pulls on the energy you have and isn't helpful to sustaining a supportive and grounded environment.

Your kitchen and jar are a reflection of where your healing is in this moment. Every time you take a step forward, things rearrange and change based on your needs and desires. Even when you're choosing something that you don't really want, things still shift and move around. To believe that we will reach a point where we won't need to make adjustments to our lives is to put a large amount of pressure on ourselves to get healing done right, and like science, healing is an opportunity to explore, gather evidence, and then make decisions based on what we learn. And things are always changing, and honestly, thank goodness for that, right? We wouldn't want things to be stuck at the level of healing we were at five years ago, five months ago, or even before you finished this book.

And we don't want healing to become a space where we set really unrealistic expectations for ourselves and are consistently let down when we can't meet them, even though before we set them we knew that it wasn't possible. Not because we're not capable, but because healing has no metric or rubric system. We make the rules. Do I feel good? Okay, I'll keep going in this direction. Do I feel burned out, overwhelmed, tired most of the time, and irritable? Okay, I need to take a break and figure out what needs to change so that I get back to feeling good.

WHEN DID YOU KNOW
YOU WERE HEALING?

A big part of the way I teach self-healing is ensuring that people understand that the responsibility of healing is on you. No one can heal you for you. You're entrusted and liable for committing to that work for yourself long-term. But the beauty of owning your healing and being responsible for the journey is that you also get to name and declare, to yourself or to others that you trust, when you know for sure that you **are** healing.

So when did you begin to recognize that you were healing? Did you notice that you were able to stand up for yourself more often?

Did you ask questions before you committed to something? Were you willing to not always get it right because you've begun to accept that mistakes are a part of life? Were you able to let love in? Did you learn how to accept compliments?

There are so many different ways that we can tell that we're healing, and it's not through our perfectionism or ability to get it right. We can tell that we're healing through the small and big ways that we choose ourselves. Each time we decide to be there for ourselves, we **know** we're healing. And it doesn't mean that we'll do it every single time. Having the grace for that is also healing.

ASK YOURSELF:

- When did I know I was healing?

And then write:

- I knew I was healing when I learned to give myself grace.

- I knew I was healing when I chose my joy over their comfort.

- I knew I was healing when . . .

I invite you to add this to your weekly journaling or self-healing practice. It's important to remind yourself of how the work you're doing is paying off. Even understanding that what you're currently doing isn't working is healing because you're aware of your needs. Healing is an educational journey where we are continuously learning more about what we need, who we are, and how the world impacts us as everything moves, shifts, changes, and grows. Healing has no graduation. We may be done with certain cycles, certain unhealthy people, or certain harmful behavior, and that's amazing and should definitely be celebrated. But as we grow, as people come and go, and as things change we'll have different needs and therefore also require different healing tools, too.

This isn't evidence of your brokenness, as you're not broken. This is a part of being human. We will spend our lives taking gentle care of ourselves and the people we care about and this is an amazing honor, in my opinion. To get to care for yourself and to know that you need care is a blessing. To not know what you need but to care enough to find out is also a blessing. It gets tough working through similar cycles and situations that you wish you didn't have to go through. Sometimes we choose tough circumstances and sometimes tough circumstances happen to us. But either way, we can connect to our healing and be there for ourselves every step of the way. Remembering that our sugar is valuable. Remembering that our jars can break, but will always mend. Remembering that we get to decide what we need from moment to moment. And making the space and time to sit comfortably in the coziest corner of our kitchen and just be.

11

PRACTICE FILLING
YOUR JAR

When I was in high school, my favorite thing to do on the way to school was to put a new CD in my CD player and listen to it from beginning to end. Because I commuted from Brooklyn to Queens for school, I was on the F train for more than an hour on a good day. And then on a bus for another thirty minutes or so. This meant that I could listen to a full album with pretty much no skipping! One particular morning, I jumped off the bus, stepping carefully onto the sidewalk to escape the dirty grayish-brown snow waiting at my feet. I was listening to *The Blueprint* album, by Jay-Z, when my CD player stopped, and whether it was because the album had ended or my batteries died, I kept my hands in the very cozy pockets of my North Face jacket, because it was far too cold to find out.

But the album wasn't done. A bonus track started playing, and I literally felt like I'd hit the jackpot. I stayed outside the school so that I could listen a little longer because we couldn't wear headphones inside. That afternoon when school was dismissed and I started the trek to the bus stop for my after-school job, I skipped all the way to the last song on the album so that I could hear the bonus track again. And to my surprise, after the first bonus track ended, another one began! I felt like it was only me who knew this! I loved discovering that and to this day I always let all songs play out completely because you never know when a bonus track is waiting.

I hope this section of the book gives you those same feelings that I felt when I got to the end of an album and found that there was more waiting for me. These activities were created to help you dig even deeper into your sugar jar, even after you're done reading the book. Repeat these exercises anytime you need to reassess your sugar jar or your kitchen.

HOW'S YOUR JAR?

How's your sugar jar? Right at this moment. Where does your sugar go every day? What responsibilities are on your mind? What keeps you up at night? What distracts you while you're doing something else? What do you worry about? Where are you lacking support or care?

EXAMPLES

- Finances.

- Romantic relationship.

- Children.

- Divorce.

- Physical healing.

- Toxic family relationships/friendships.

- Self-care.

- Watching TV.

- Working.

YOUR MEASUREMENTS

- How much sugar does each of these tasks take from your jar (e.g., work takes how many cups of sugar)?

- How much sugar do these activities put back into your jar?

YOUR DREAM JAR

- What would your jar look like if you could make it any way you wanted?

- What can you do to get your jar closer to looking like this rather than the jar you have now?

- What about your jar do you currently enjoy?

SIGNS AND REMINDERS
THAT YOU'RE HEALING

Write down signs and reminders that you're healing.

- I know I'm healing . . .

- What do I do differently than I did before?

- What do I say no to that I would've been afraid to speak out about before?

SIMPLE REMINDERS

- Remember, you're allowed to slow down.

- You're allowed to procrastinate if you need to.

- You're allowed to ask for help.

- Remember, acceptance and blame are not the same.

- You're allowed to make mistakes.

- You're not doing it wrong.

- You don't always have to be doing something.

FILL YOUR JAR

Write down activities that fill your jar so that you have a list to turn to when you need it.

EXAMPLES

- Taking a long walk.

- Laughing on FaceTime with a friend.

- Making an elaborate meal.

- Drinking tea.

- Spending time outside.

- Getting acupuncture.

- Taking CBD.

- Taking a nap.

- Meditating.

- Trying something new or exciting.

- Decluttering.

KITCHEN RENO

Sometimes, after tending to your jar, you look around your kitchen and realize that it's a little outdated for your new tastes. Not. to. worry.

You can remodel! And it can feel like a big job, but remember, it's your kitchen. This project can be as slow or fast as you'd like and as small or big as you're comfortable with, and as a reminder, you'll be making updates for life. So just do what feels good now knowing you can make changes whenever you choose to.

Let's get some clarity on design:

- What feels good about your kitchen? Do you like who has access? Would you like there to be more light? Do you have a cozy corner where you can take space to be?

Now let's think about the space:

- What do you think about the size of your kitchen? Is it big enough to hold everyone and everything that has access to it?

Finally, what's already here that you'd like to keep and what do you know needs to go as it no longer fits "the new decor"?

What's important to remember is that you get to renovate your kitchen, change out your jar for a larger or smaller size, or perhaps even change the lid of your jar from a screw-on top to a lid with a clamp closure. You get to decide what your life looks like, what's comfortable, what no longer works, what dreams you want to make a reality, or what dreams you're living that you've realized aren't what you want. The power is in your hands. No matter whom you have in your life. You get to choose.

FINAL THOUGHTS

When I first started talking publicly about the Sugar Jar and teaching its concepts, I honestly thought it would be a one-time-and-done kind of thing. And then each time I would meet someone new they would always bring the Sugar Jar up. That didn't annoy me, but looking back, I recognize that there was a part of me that was running from my own work. I'm a huge believer in practicing what you teach, and not from a place of perfection anymore, but from a place of honesty. And there were still a few places in my life where I wasn't ready to close my lid even though it was absolutely draining me and negatively affecting my well-being. I wanted to walk away from the Sugar Jar because I didn't want to deal with my jar. Haven't we all been there? But everything changed after teaching it in person for the first time.

I'd just finished teaching my first sugar jar workshop. After workshops you get to connect with the audience as they come over to share their thoughts, ideas, beliefs, or even criticisms. It's honestly my favorite part of the whole workshop process because we've all just journeyed together and now we can talk about all the things we saw or experienced along the way.

A woman walked up to me and excitedly said, "I've got to tell you this story, you honestly won't believe my sugar jar story." As this was only my first sugar jar workshop and I'd only previously taught it as a sugar jar challenge via my newsletter, I was nervous and excited to hear what she would say. She goes, "I joined your first sugar jar challenge last year and I knew my sugar was all over the place. I'm thinking to myself, 'Who the hell is going to help me clean this up? I didn't make this mess, why am I responsible for doing the dirty work alone?'"

I nodded in agreement because, whew, have I been there. We all have.

"And as I'm figuring out this sugar jar situation, I get a text from my boss on a Saturday asking me to check my email as soon as I get the chance because it's urgent. But it's always urgent. Mind you, I don't work weekends. I don't get paid for weekends. And I instantly felt this anxiety in my throat . . ." She trailed off as tears started to run down her face. We were holding hands now. "I want to be able to say no. I want to be able to live my life, too. But everyone always asks me, everyone always expects me, everyone always comes to me, and I always give because I love big. But I'm tired. I am tired."

She took a deep breath and laughed while apologizing for "taking up too much time," and I replied, "You don't have to apologize for giving yourself what you need in this moment. You get to be filled, too. You get to receive, too." We nodded and smiled at each other as she thanked me for the workshop, and then we headed in our separate directions.

A few months later, I received a message from her sharing, "Hey, Yasmine! I just wanted to let you know that after our talk, I didn't answer my boss's text. I was scared because I need my job, but I didn't reply until Monday. My boss didn't say anything for a while, and then during our first meeting, they asked me why I didn't answer their *urgent* message that I got. I let them know that it was a weekend and I needed to make sure that I wasn't working 24/7 for my mental health. I was so proud of myself. Unfortunately, my boss was not. I didn't lose my job, but they kept messaging me and doing things that made me feel unvalued. I felt like I was doing this 'self-healing' thing wrong, because I thought they'd get me and understand what I was saying about taking care of myself. But I remembered that other people won't always get me. It sucks to receive them, but I still don't answer those messages on the weekend. And it's the first time I've ever chosen me."

When I saw her message, I realized that the Sugar Jar wasn't just a workshop, or a podcast, or even a book. It was a movement. And it wouldn't always be easy, right? Of course, I was running from my jar, we all do it at one time or another. We've all experienced the uncomfortable realization that we need to make decisions for our betterment that may have tough consequences for those we need space from. And there's often some time between that moment of awareness and our ability to decide what we're going to do next. The brave and kind thing we can do for ourselves in those in-between moments is to continue to tend to our jars and kitchens until we know what we'll choose. While we figure it out, we can sweep up the spilled sugar, knowing that we'll be there for ourselves even in the mess of it. Because we don't have to run from this work, which is something I've learned again and again.

It might be uncomfortable. It might take time. And it might take a new kind of strength that doesn't require that we pretend all is well when it isn't. That's the beauty of knowing that we **can** get it wrong. We learn, then we know, and then we grow. And then we do it all over again. But we keep choosing and we keep coming back to ourselves and thank goodness for that.

Make room to enjoy the sweet parts of life. The sweet parts of you.

ACKNOWLEDGMENTS

I am so grateful to my children and husband, who supported me while I needed the free space to create this book. Thank you for always being excited when I came down after my writing sessions. I love you all so much.

To Nikki + Miko, "the best nights of our lives" are still arriving, lol. Thanks so much for your encouragement and consistent excitement throughout this process. Thanks for riding with me forever.

To my mom, who was the first version of creative entrepreneurship that I ever witnessed up close. Thank you for showing me that when you believe in something, you **can** do it.

To my grandmother, thank you for always thinking of me. Always. For allowing me to come into your kitchen and get cozy. For always saving some sugar for me.

To Leigh, thank you for believing in what was possible for me! For partnering with me when no one else wanted to and for answering each question with such kindness. For seeing my vision and helping me bring it to life. You are amazing, and I'm so grateful for you.

To Anna, thank you for allowing me to bring this vision to life.

You are a gift, and I'm so grateful I got you as my partner on this journey.

To HarperOne, thank you for believing in me.

To Alex, Nedra, and Layla—thank you for believing in this book. I am so grateful to you.

ABOUT THE AUTHOR

Yasmine Cheyenne is a self-healing educator and mental-wellness advocate who helps people learn how to cultivate daily practices to build healthy, joyful lives. Corporate giants including ABC, Meta, and Skillshare have invited her to share her transformative teachings around self-healing, which she also offers through keynote speeches, corporate presentations, and one-on-one coaching. Her instruction has helped tens of thousands of students take control of their financial and physical health by creating boundaries, designing their dream job, finding the love of their life, and more.

Yasmine brings to her practice more than fifteen years of legal and business experience, including being in the Air Force JAG on active duty and working in the Department of Veterans Affairs. She has helped victims of domestic violence and sexual assault. Yasmine owns The Sugar Jar® Community app, which provides accessible self-healing tools for everyone, and she's the host of her own podcast, *The Sugar Jar Podcast*. Her expertise has been featured on *The Today Show* and in *Forbes* and *InStyle*. She lives outside of Washington, DC, with her husband and two children.